SOUPS

SOUPS

Over 200 of the best recipes

hamlyn

First published in Great Britain in 2007 by
Hamlyn, a division of Octopus Publishing Group Ltd,
2–4 Heron Quays, London E14 4JP

Published in 2007 by Sterling Publishing Co., Inc.
387 Park Avenue South, New York, NY 10016

Distributed in Canada by Sterling Publishing
c/o Canadian Manda Group, 165 Dufferin Street
Toronto, Ontario, Canada M6K 3H6

ISBN-13: 978-0-600-61711-2
ISBN-10: 0-600-61711-4

A CIP catalog record for this book is available
from the British Library

Printed and bound in China

10 9 8 7 6 5 4 3 2 1

Notes
This book includes dishes made with nuts and nut derivatives. It is advisable for those with known allergic
reactions to nuts and nut derivatives and those who may be potentially vulnerable to these allergies, such as
pregnant and nursing mothers, invalids, the elderly, babies, and children, to avoid dishes made with nuts
and nut oils. It is also prudent to check the labels of preprepared ingredients for the possible inclusion of
nut derivatives.

The Food and Drug Administration advises that eggs should not be consumed raw. This book contains some
dishes made with raw or lightly cooked eggs. It is prudent for more vulnerable people such as pregnant and
nursing mothers, invalids, the elderly, babies, and young children to avoid uncooked or lightly cooked
dishes made with eggs.

Meat and poultry should be cooked thoroughly. To test if poultry is cooked, pierce the flesh through the
thickest part with a skewer or fork—the juices should run clear, never pink or red.

Ovens should be preheated to the specified temperature. If using a fan-assisted oven, follow the
manufacturer's instructions for adjusting the time and temperature. Broilers should also be preheated.

contents

introduction

When it comes to quick, convenient, and nutritious meals, a bowl of soup and a fresh crusty roll are the perfect solution. From hearty winter soups to clear broths and refreshing, chilled gazpachos, soup is extremely versatile and can be enjoyed whenever you feel like a speedy snack or an easy lunch or evening meal.

A hot bowl of homemade soup is the ultimate comfort food, and it can be extremely quick to prepare. Simply make large batches of your favorite recipe and keep it in the refrigerator for a day or two, or freeze it for later use. This way you can still enjoy a delicious meal even when you're really short of time or are too tired to prepare a meal from scratch. Some freshly chopped herbs or a handful of grated cheese will add the perfect finishing touch.

Some ingredients naturally work well together, and soup is the ideal way to enjoy these special combinations. Each has a unique flavor when cooked separately, but when they are simmered together in one pan, they merge to produce a very different taste. **Chicken and Corn Soup** (see page 45), **Pea and Mint Soup** (see page 123), **New Potato, Cilantro, and Leek Soup** (see page 126), and **Melon and Prosciutto Soup** (see page 251) are just some of the recipes in this book that use ingredients that work well together. However, you will also discover more unusual partners that result in surprising, but equally enjoyable, soups. **Spicy Apple and Potato Soup** (see page 128) and **Garlic and Almond Soup** (see page 224) are just a couple of examples.

In the following chapters you will find more than 200 soup recipes for every occasion and to suit every palate. Whether you have minutes or hours to create your soup, you will be spoilt for choice, and there are plenty of ideas for impressive dinner party starters as well as quick lunches. You will also find tips on preparing garnishes, a checklist of the equipment you will need, and recipes for the basic stocks that are used in many of the soups in this book.

Soup through the ages

Soup was probably a regular fixture on the dinner menu as soon as ancient people had learned how to make fire and fashion a vessel in which to contain liquid. Many foods, including a large number of seeds and plants, are inedible unless they have been boiled, and this cooking method would have provided people with a more plentiful and varied diet. Although the cooking liquid may well have been secondary to the actual food in the pot, it would have represented a warming and nutritious drink. Over time, as an understanding of the ingredients developed, it was realized that otherwise bland—but nutritious—foods could be combined with more flavorsome ingredients to create interesting meals.

During the Middle Ages, soup was a popular dish, and the introduction of new and unusual ingredients from further afield led to the development of a good variety of vegetable and meat broths and soups. Soup could be prepared in advance and left to its own devices while the cook of the household got on with other courses.

Originally, soup would have been poured over bread before being eaten, and this is one of the theories about the origin of the word "soup," because the drenched bread was referred to as "sop."

Eventually, however, soup began to be appreciated as a dish in its own right and was consumed directly from the bowl. As spoons were a relatively late addition to the dining table, this would have involved drinking it. The large bowl of soup would be passed around, with each person taking a few sips and maybe helping themselves to a chunk of meat or whatever ingredients had been cooked in the simmering liquid.

Throughout history, soup has been regarded as a suitable food for invalids, presumably because a warm broth is easy to consume and digest, and the dish could easily be adjusted to include particularly health-promoting foods. Even today, a comforting bowl of hot chicken soup is a favorite treatment for sufferers from colds and flu, and it is the food we turn to when we are feeling low or in need of a lift.

Home comforts

There is something comforting about a big saucepan of homemade soup simmering away on the stove. Even if you aren't particularly confident in the kitchen, you will be able to create delicious, simple soups using fresh ingredients and enjoy the benefits of tucking into a homemade meal. Any produce you happen to have in your kitchen can generally be transformed into a tasty soup, and making a soup is a great way of using up odd vegetables or meat left over from the Sunday roast. The best thing about homemade soup is that you know exactly what's going into it, so you can keep it as wholesome as you like.

Although there are many great soup varieties available to buy these days, there isn't a lot of effort involved in making your own. You can pick your flavor, adding more or less of certain ingredients depending on what you have available, and one session in the kitchen could result in enough soup for weeks. Buy some freezer-proof cartons or use food bags to freeze individual portions, so you only have to defrost the amount you need.

You can choose your recipes to reflect seasonally available ingredients and enjoy soup all year round. Although we traditionally regard soup as a winter dish, light broths and chilled soups can make a refreshing meal for a warm summer's day. In fact, a whole chapter is devoted to chilled soups in the book, with delicious recipes, such as **Iced Tomato Soup with Salsa Verde** (see page 235) and **Chilled Watercress Soup** (see page 238), offering you the satisfaction of creating appetizing dishes using the best local produce.

A healthy option

As well as often being a quick and simple meal, soup can also be a healthy choice. We all know that we're supposed to eat at least five portions of fresh fruit and vegetables every day, but this isn't always easy. Busy lifestyles or long hours in the office often mean that our diet suffers, and it's easy to resort to unhealthy snacks and ready-prepared meals when we're stressed or don't have much time to cook. Many of the recipes in this book include a varied selection of vegetables as well as fresh herbs, fragrant spices, legumes, seafood, and poultry. A bowl of soup can be a well-balanced meal, and you also have the enjoyment of tucking into a homemade dish, which will always taste better than something from a package or can.

The cooking techniques used to make soup mean that more of the valuable nutrients remain in the finished dish. Soup is often a one-pot meal with vegetables cooked in the stock, rather than in a separate pan, from which the cooking water—along with many of the vitamins—is discarded when the vegetables are boiled and strained. In most soup recipes, raw vegetables will simply be added to the stock or cooked in a little oil before the liquid is added. This is also a great way to cook legumes, and you'll find lentils, peas, and beans in many recipes. Legumes are a rich source of protein and fiber, so they are a good choice for vegetarians and also a nutritious way of bulking up soup to make a more filling meal. Some dried legumes need presoaking, but others can be added directly to the soup, absorbing the flavors from the stock.

back to basics

The great thing about making soup is that you don't really need to buy any specialist equipment. A well-stocked kitchen will already contain everything you need to make most of the recipes in this book, but here's a rundown of the basics so that you can make sure that you have the necessary items to hand.

Set of saucepans

If you cook regularly, you will already have a selection of good-quality saucepans. It's worth spending as much as you can afford because you will then get a product that should last you for years. You will need a large, heavy saucepan for the actual soup as well as a smaller one for heating stocks and cooking other ingredients. A small, nonstick skillet will also come in useful.

 ## Sharp knives

You will need a large knife for chopping vegetables and smaller knives for filleting, cutting up smaller vegetables, and for dicing meat.

 ## Ladle

You will need a ladle for serving the soup, whether you are transferring it from the saucepan direct to soup bowls or serving at the table where the soup is presented in a decorative tureen.

 ## Blender or food processor

Many soups are partly blended, and sometimes the whole soup is blended, so a blender or food processor will prove useful if you're planning to make lots of soup. A food processor is also useful as a quick, effortless way of chopping onions and other vegetables. If you don't have a food processor, an immersion blender should be sufficient for most recipes. You might also find a potato masher useful, because some recipes call for soups to be lightly mashed or blended to give them a coarse texture.

 ## Ice-cube trays

You can use these to store small amounts of soup, and they are also good for storing stock. This means that you can make a large amount and then use a number of cubes, depending on the amount of soup you're preparing at the time.

finishing touches

Because soup is such a versatile dish, you may be serving it for anything from a quick family meal to an impressive appetizer for a dinner party. In fact, soup is a great choice when you have guests because most of the preparation, and often the cooking, can be done in advance. To make your dish look even more impressive, there are plenty of lovely ideas for garnishes and toppings. Add these to the bowls just before serving to ensure that they stay fresh and crisp.

 Herbs

Fresh herbs add color and flavor to soups, and you should try to match the herbs used for the garnish to those used in the main recipe. A couple of long chives carefully placed across the center of the bowl can look very effective, or you could try a dollop of crème fraîche, topped with some snipped chives. Whole basil leaves work well on tomato-based soups, while chopped fresh cilantro adds a cool contrast to spicy flavors.

 Cream

Many soups contain milk or cream, and it's nice to finish these off with a swirl of cream on top. Cream also works well with zucchini or tomato soups. A small spoonful of plain yogurt, crème fraîche or sour cream could be used as an alternative. A pinch of paprika can add a colorful contrast to the white crème fraîche and would work well with hearty flavors or spicy soups.

Croutons

You can buy packets of croutons if you're really pressed for time, but it's easy to make your own. Simply cut the crusts from a couple of slices of thick, white bread and cut the bread into even-sized squares (you can make these as small or big as you like). Place them on a lightly greased baking sheet and brush them with a little olive oil. Bake them in a preheated medium-hot oven, 400°F, for 8–10 minutes or until they are crisp and golden. For a variation, sprinkle with a little grated Parmesan cheese or cut the bread into long, thin strips instead. You can even use cookie cutters to create different shapes.

Very thin slices of baguette also work well with grated cheese. You can broil these until the cheese has melted and balance one or two on top of each bowl of soup. Alternatively, you can rub bread with garlic as in Onion Soup with Garlic Croutons (see page 112).

Bread

Instead of the traditional bread roll, you could try toasting pita breads and cutting them into slices. Arrange these on a plate to serve with the soup. Thin strips of warmed naan bread or flour tortilla are also good for dunking.

Other ideas

Try balancing a couple of slices of crisp bacon on the soup. Seafood soups look impressive with one or two large shrimp in the center. Very finely chopped onion and tomato make a great finish for chilled summer soups, and a little grated orange zest will add a zing to any soups that include orange juice.

Fish stock

2 tablespoons **butter**

3 **shallots**, roughly chopped

1 small **leek**, roughly chopped

1 **celery stick** or piece of **fennel**, roughly chopped

2 lb **white fish** or **shellfish bones, heads, and trimmings**

⅔ cup **dry white wine**

several sprigs of **parsley**

½ **lemon**, sliced

1 teaspoon **black peppercorns** or **white peppercorns**

4 cups **water**

10

PREP

30

COOK

4 cups

MAKES

Do not use oily fish to make stock because it will make it greasy and give it an overpowering flavor. Fish stock requires less cooking than meat stocks, so take care that you do not overcook it or you will spoil the flavor.

1 Melt the butter in a large, heavy aucepan until bubbling.

2 Add all the vegetables and cook over a moderate heat for 5 minutes or until softened but not browned. Add the fish bones, heads and trimmings, wine, parsley, lemon, peppercorns, and measured water.

3 Bring to a boil, skimming off the scum that rises to the surface. Reduce the heat and simmer the stock for 20 minutes.

4 Strain, cover, and allow to cool. Chill in the refrigerator overnight, then remove and discard the layer of fat that will have set on the surface. Store in the refrigerator for up to 24 hours or freeze immediately.

Chicken stock

PREP 10

COOK 120

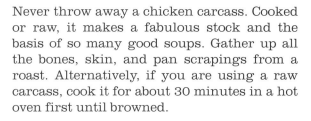

Never throw away a chicken carcass. Cooked or raw, it makes a fabulous stock and the basis of so many good soups. Gather up all the bones, skin, and pan scrapings from a roast. Alternatively, if you are using a raw carcass, cook it for about 30 minutes in a hot oven first until browned.

4 cups

MAKES

1 large **chicken carcass**, including any trimmings, such as the neck, heart, and gizzard if available (but not the liver)

1 **onion**, roughly chopped

1 large **carrot**, roughly chopped

several **bay leaves**

1 teaspoon **black peppercorns**

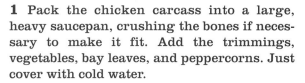

1 Pack the chicken carcass into a large, heavy saucepan, crushing the bones if necessary to make it fit. Add the trimmings, vegetables, bay leaves, and peppercorns. Just cover with cold water.

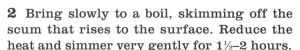

2 Bring slowly to a boil, skimming off the scum that rises to the surface. Reduce the heat and simmer very gently for 1½–2 hours.

3 Strain, cover, and allow to cool. Chill in the refrigerator overnight, then remove and discard the layer of fat that will have set on the surface. Store in the refrigerator for up to 4 days or freeze immediately.

Beef stock

15
PREP

300
COOK

3½ lb **beef bones**, chopped into 3 inch pieces

2 **onions**, quartered

2 **carrots**, chopped

2 **celery sticks**, chopped

2 **tomatoes**, chopped

4 quarts **water**

10 sprigs of **parsley**

4 sprigs of **thyme**

2 **bay leaves**

8 **black peppercorns**

8
cups

MAKES

When you buy beef, remember to get the bones as well and ask the butcher to cut them into manageable pieces. You can use cheaper cuts of beef and trimmings instead, but that's more expensive than using bones.

1 Put the bones in a large roasting pan and roast in a preheated oven, 450°F, for 30 minutes or until lightly browned and the fat and juices run, turning occasionally. Add all the vegetables, spoon over the fat from the pan, and roast, stirring occasionally, for an additional 30 minutes.

2 Transfer the bones and vegetables to a large, heavy saucepan. Pour off the fat from the pan and add ⅔ cup of the measured water. Set over a low heat and bring to a boil, scraping up any sediment. Pour into the saucepan. Add the remaining water.

3 Bring to a boil, skimming off the scum that rises to the surface. Add the herbs and peppercorns. Partially cover, then reduce the heat and simmer for 4 hours.

4 Strain, cover, and allow to cool. Chill in the refrigerator overnight, then remove and discard the layer of fat that will have set on the surface. Store in the refrigerator for up to 4 days or freeze immediately.

Vegetable stock

You can use any combination of vegetables that you like, but make sure that they are fresh. Always include onions, but avoid any with strong flavors, such as cabbage, and starchy ones, such as potatoes, which will make the stock cloudy. In many of the recipes you can use chicken stock instead.

1 Melt the butter in a large, heavy saucepan, add all the vegetables and stir well to coat, then cover and cook over a low heat for 10 minutes.

2 Stir in all the herbs and add the measured water. Bring to a boil, then reduce the heat, cover, and simmer for 15 minutes.

3 Strain the stock, cover, and allow to cool. Chill in the refrigerator overnight. Store the stock in the refrigerator for up to 2 days or freeze immediately.

15

PREP

30

COOK

2½ cups

MAKES

¼ cup **butter**

2 **onions**, chopped

2 **leeks**, thinly sliced

2 **carrots**, chopped

2 **celery sticks**, chopped

1 **fennel bulb**, chopped

1 sprig of **thyme**

1 sprig of **marjoram**

1 sprig of **fennel**

4 sprigs of **parsley**

4 cups **water**

meat and poultry

½ cup **butter**

5 oz **pancetta** or **bacon**, chopped

2 **onions**, finely chopped

1 **carrot**, chopped

1 **celery stick**, chopped

1½ lb can **whole chestnuts**, drained and rinsed

1 tablespoon chopped **rosemary**

2 **bay leaves**

2 **garlic cloves**, halved

salt and **pepper**

sprigs of **rosemary**, to garnish

20

PREP

60

COOK

6

SERVES

herby

Chestnut soup with pancetta and rosemary

We tend to think of chestnuts as a Christmas delicacy, but they are available canned, so you can use them all year round. They add a lovely woody flavor to dishes.

1 Melt the butter in a large, heavy saucepan, add the pancetta or bacon and cook over a moderate heat until starting to brown. Add the onions, carrot, and celery and cook for 5–10 minutes or until softened and browned.

2 Add the chestnuts, rosemary, bay leaves, and garlic to the pan. Add enough water to cover completely and bring to a boil. Partially cover, reduce the heat, and simmer, stirring occasionally, for 30 minutes. The chestnuts should start to disintegrate and thicken the soup. Taste and season well with salt and pepper.

3 Ladle the soup into warm bowls and serve garnished with rosemary sprigs.

Potato and bacon soup

The bacon rind is left on in this recipe because the fat adds lots of flavor to the soup. Always use proper stocks in soups—they are far superior to those made up from bouillon cubes.

20

PREP

60

COOK

8

SERVES

tasty

1 Cut the rind off the bacon and set aside. Chop the bacon roughly. Heat the oil in a large, heavy saucepan, add the rind and cook over a moderate heat until crisp. Remove with a slotted spoon and discard.

2 Add the chopped bacon, onion, and garlic to the bacon fat and cook over a moderate heat, stirring frequently, for 8–10 minutes or until the onion is lightly browned and the bacon fairly crisp.

3 Add the stock, measured water, potatoes, leeks, marjoram, nutmeg, Worcestershire sauce, and pepper to taste. Bring to a boil, then reduce the heat, cover, and simmer, stirring occasionally, for 25 minutes.

4 In a blender or food processor, blend 2½ cups of the soup for 2 seconds. Return to the pan. Stir well and simmer gently for an additional 10 minutes. Season to taste with salt and pepper. Stir in the parsley (if using) and serve immediately in warm soup bowls.

6 oz **bacon**, rind on

1 tablespoon **olive oil**

1 **onion**, finely chopped

2 **garlic cloves**, finely chopped

2½ cups **Chicken Stock** (see page 17)

5 cups **water**

1½ lb **potatoes**, diced

3 **leeks**, sliced

1 teaspoon chopped **marjoram**

¼ teaspoon **grated nutmeg**

1 teaspoon **Worcestershire sauce**

3–4 tablespoons finely chopped **parsley** (optional)

salt and **pepper**

1 teaspoon **olive oil**

2 slices of **bacon**, chopped

2 **garlic cloves**, crushed

1 **onion**, chopped

few sprigs of **thyme** or **lemon thyme**

2 x 13 oz cans **cannellini beans**, rinsed and drained

2½ cups **Vegetable Stock** (see page 19)

2 tablespoons chopped **parsley**

pepper

crusty **bread**, to serve

5

PREP

15

COOK

4

SERVES

quick

Smoky bacon and white bean soup

Beans and other legumes make a wonderful addition to soups. Not only do they add bulk, but they also absorb the flavors from other ingredients. Canned beans are great to use for convenience, but you could soak dried beans and use those, if you prefer.

1 Heat the oil in a large, heavy saucepan, add the bacon, garlic, and onion and cook over a moderate heat for about 3–4 minutes or until the bacon is beginning to brown and the onion to soften.

2 Add the thyme or lemon thyme and cook for an additional 1 minute. Add the beans and stock and bring to a boil, then reduce the heat and simmer for 10 minutes.

3 In a blender or food processor, blend the soup with the parsley and pepper to taste until smooth. Return to the pan and reheat gently. Serve the soup in warm bowls with crusty bread.

Bacon and turnip soup

15

PREP

45

COOK

6

SERVES

thick

The humble turnip has suffered from neglect in kitchens in recent years, but this hearty vegetable is perfect for soups, stews, and casseroles. Here, it complements the rich, salty taste of the bacon.

1 Melt the butter in a large, heavy saucepan, add the bacon and cook over a moderate heat until crisp and golden. Remove with a slotted spoon and reserve.

2 Add the onion, potatoes, and turnips to the bacon fat and cook over a low heat for about 5 minutes. Add the stock, bay leaf, and thyme and bring to a boil, then reduce the heat and cook for 30–35 minutes or until all the vegetables are tender. Remove and discard the bay leaf and thyme.

3 In a blender or food processor, blend the soup in batches until smooth, then transfer it to a clean saucepan. Add the reserved bacon and the milk and reheat gently without boiling. Serve the soup in warm soup bowls, sprinkled with a little finely chopped parsley.

2 tablespoons **butter**

4 oz rindless **bacon**, roughly chopped

1 **onion**, roughly chopped

12 oz **potatoes**, chopped

1½ lb **turnips**, chopped

5 cups **Chicken Stock** (see page 17)

1 **bay leaf**

1 small sprig of **thyme**

⅔ cup **milk**

salt and **pepper**

finely chopped **parsley**, to garnish

2 tablespoons **olive oil**

3 slices of **bacon**, chopped

2 **onions**, finely chopped

2½ cups **Chicken Stock** (see page 17)

4 cups **water**

1¼ lb **potatoes**, cut into ½ inch cubes

4 tablespoons **all-purpose flour**

2 oz **Gruyère cheese**, grated

1 tablespoon **medium dry sherry**

1 teaspoon **Worcestershire sauce**

3 tablespoons finely chopped **parsley**

salt and **pepper**

20
PREP

30
COOK

6
SERVES

tasty

Gruyère soup with bacon and potatoes

Parsley makes the perfect garnish for this rich, flavorful soup, giving it a touch of vibrant color and a contrasting crispness.

1 Heat the oil in a large, heavy saucepan, add the bacon and onions and cook over a moderate heat until the onion is pale golden. Add the stock, 2½ cups of the measured water, and the potatoes and bring to a boil, reduce the heat, cover, and simmer for 15 minutes or until the potatoes are tender.

2 In a small bowl, beat the flour with the remaining water and stir the mixture into the soup. Cover and simmer, stirring frequently, for an additional 5 minutes.

3 In a blender or food processor, blend the Gruyère with 1¼ cups of the soup. Return to the pan and add the sherry, Worcestershire sauce, and pepper to taste. Simmer for 3–5 minutes. Stir in the parsley and serve immediately in warm soup bowls.

Green lentil and bacon soup

Also known as French lentils, green lentils are, as the name suggests, popular in European cooking, and they make a wholesome soup that is a good source of protein. Unlike orange and brown lentils, which quickly cook down to a puree, green lentils retain their shape after cooking.

1 Melt the butter in a large, heavy saucepan, add the bacon, garlic, and onion and cook over a moderate to high heat for 5 minutes.

2 Reduce the heat and add the lentils, celery, carrot, parsley, thyme, and bay leaf to the pan. Pour in the stock and measured water and bring to a boil, skimming off the scum that rises to the surface. Add the lemon slice.

3 Reduce the heat, cover, and simmer, stirring occasionally, for 55–60 minutes. Add a little more water if the soup is too thick. Remove and discard the parsley, thyme, bay leaf, and lemon slice.

4 In a blender or food processor, blend 2½ cups of the soup until smooth. Return to the pan, stir well, and season to taste with salt and pepper. Reheat gently. Transfer to warm soup bowls and serve immediately.

20

PREP

75

COOK

6

SERVES

hearty

2 tablespoons **butter**

4 oz rindless **bacon**, finely chopped

1 **garlic clove**, finely chopped

1 **onion**, finely chopped

1¾ cups **green lentils**, washed and drained

1 **celery stick**, sliced

1 large **carrot**, diced

1 sprig of **parsley**

1 sprig of **thyme**

1 **bay leaf**

5 cups **Chicken Stock** (see page 17)

4 cups **water**

1 slice of **lemon**

salt and **pepper**

1½ cups **yellow split peas**, soaked overnight in cold water

2 tablespoons **olive oil**

3 **chorizo sausages**, thinly sliced

1 **onion**, chopped

2 **garlic cloves**, finely chopped

5 cups **Chicken Stock** (see page 17)

4 cups **water**

1 **bay leaf**

1 sprig of **thyme**

3 **carrots**, quartered lengthwise and thinly sliced

salt

20*

PREP

120

COOK

6

SERVES

spicy

Yellow pea soup with chorizo

Chorizo is a spicy sausage, originating from Spain and Latin America, made with pork and seasoned with garlic, paprika, and hot peppers. It gives this traditional legume-based soup a special bite.

1 Drain the soaked split peas, rinse under cold running water, and drain again.

2 Heat the oil in a large, heavy saucepan, add the chorizo and cook over a moderate heat for 5 minutes or until browned. Remove with a slotted spoon and leave to drain on paper towels. Pour off all but 1 tablespoon of the fat in the pan.

3 Add the onion and garlic to the pan and cook over a moderate heat for 5 minutes or until softened. Add the split peas, stock, measured water, bay leaf, and thyme and bring to a boil, skimming off the scum that rises to the surface. Reduce the heat, partially cover, and simmer, stirring occasionally, for 1¼ hours.

4 Add the carrots and cook for an additional 30 minutes or until tender. Season to taste with salt. Remove and discard the bay leaf, add the reserved chorizo, and cook for an additional 10 minutes. Serve immediately in warm, deep soup bowls.

* Plus overnight soaking

Beef and noodle broth

This nourishing soup relies on good, well-flavored stock and is ideal for using up any beef or chicken stock that you might have in the freezer. When you are slicing the beef, cut it across the grain so that it falls into tender, succulent slices.

1 Trim any fat from the beef. Mix the ginger with 1 teaspoon of the soy sauce and smooth over both sides of the beef.

2 Cook the rice noodles according to the package instructions. Drain and rinse under cold running water.

3 Pour the stock into a saucepan, add the chili, garlic, and sugar and bring to a gentle simmer, then cover and cook over a low heat for 5 minutes.

4 Heat the oil in a small, heavy skillet, add the beef and cook for 2 minutes on each side. Transfer to a board. When cool enough to handle, cut in half lengthwise, then cut cross into thin strips.

5 Add the noodles, sugar snap peas, basil, and remaining soy sauce to the soup and heat gently for 1 minute. Stir in the beef and serve immediately in warm soup bowls.

15
PREP

10
COOK

2
SERVES

stylish

10 oz **rump** or **sirloin steak**

½ tablespoon grated fresh **gingerroot**

2 teaspoons **light soy sauce**

2 oz dried **vermicelli rice noodles**

2½ cups **Beef Stock** (see page 18)

1 **red chili**, seeded and finely chopped

1 **garlic clove**, thinly sliced

2 teaspoons **superfine sugar**

2 teaspoons **vegetable oil**

3 oz **sugar snap peas**, halved lengthwise

small handful of **Thai basil**, torn into pieces

⅓ cup **chickpeas**, soaked overnight in cold water

¼ cup **black-eyed beans**, soaked overnight in cold water

⅓ cup **bulgar wheat**

1 lb **neck of lamb**, cut into 4 pieces

4 tablespoons **olive oil**

1 **onion**, chopped

2 **carrots**, chopped

13 oz can chopped **tomatoes**

4 small **red chilies**

4 sprigs of **thyme**

1 teaspoon each **ground coriander**, **ground cumin**, and **ground cinnamon**

½ teaspoon each **dried mint** and **dried oregano**

salt and **pepper**

TO SERVE:

olive oil

crusty **bread**

15 *

PREP

150

COOK

6

SERVES

easy

Spiced chickpea and lamb soup

The great thing about this richly spiced soup is the ease with which it is prepared and cooked. All the ingredients are put straight into a casserole (traditionally an earthenware dish) and baked until tender.

1 Drain the soaked chickpeas and beans, rinse under cold running water and drain again. Put the chickpeas and beans in separate saucepans, cover with plenty of cold water and bring to a boil. Reduce the heat and simmer for 1 hour, then drain and reserve the liquid.

2 Put the cooked chickpeas and beans in a clay pot or casserole, add all the remaining ingredients and cover with the reserved liquid. Add extra water to cover if necessary.

3 Cover the pot or casserole with a tight-fitting lid and cook in a preheated oven, 350°F, for 1½ hours or until the meat and vegetables are tender.

4 Spoon the soup into warm bowls, drizzle with olive oil, and serve accompanied with some crusty bread.

* Plus overnight soaking

Consommé

This classic soup can be served hot or chilled. If chilled, it will turn to jelly, in which case it should be broken up with a fork before being served sprinkled with finely chopped fresh herbs, such as parsley, chervil, or chives. Consommé makes an ideal appetizer if followed by a substantial second course.

1 Cut the beef into small pieces and put in a large, heavy saucepan. Add the stock, onion, celery, parsley, and peppercorns. Bring to a boil, then reduce the heat, partially cover, and simmer for 1½ hours. Carefully strain the liquid through a cheesecloth or very fine wire sieve into a separate saucepan. Add the sherry (if using).

2 To clear the consommé, add the egg white and crushed eggshell. Simmer for an additional 30 minutes, then strain again.

3 Transfer the consommé to a clean sauce-pan and add the sugar and salt (if using). Heat, stirring, until the sugar has dissolved. Serve the consommé hot or well chilled in bouillon cups.

15
PREP

120
COOK

6
SERVES

classic

12 oz lean **beef shank**

5 cups **Beef Stock** (see page 18)

1 **onion**, roughly chopped

1 **celery stick**, chopped

2 sprigs of **parsley**

6 **black peppercorns**

1 tablespoon **medium dry sherry** (optional)

1 **egg white**, lightly beaten

1 **eggshell**, lightly crushed

1 teaspoon **superfine sugar**

salt (optional)

2 lb lean **stewing beef**, cut into cubes

8 oz lean **pork**, cut into cubes

2½ quarts **water**

24 **okra**, trimmed and chopped

1 lb **kale**, stalks discarded, roughly chopped

2 **green bell peppers**, cored, seeded, and chopped

2 **scallions**, roughly chopped

1 sprig of **thyme**

¼ teaspoon **cayenne pepper**

1 lb **yellow yams**, peeled and sliced

1 large **potato**, sliced

1 **garlic clove**, finely chopped

salt

20

PREP

70

COOK

6

SERVES

exotic

Jamaican pepperpot soup

This filling, wholesome soup comes from the sunny Caribbean, but it is a perfect dish for a gloomy winter's day. Okra, sometimes known as ladies' fingers, and yams give the soup a distinctive, rather exotic flavor.

1 Combine the meat with the measured water in a large saucepan. Bring to a boil, then reduce the heat, partially cover, and simmer for about 30 minutes.

2 Add the okra, kale, bell peppers, and scallions to the soup with the thyme and cayenne pepper. Partially cover and cook over a moderate heat for 15 minutes.

3 Add the yams, potato, and garlic and cook for an additional 20 minutes or until the yams and potato are tender. Add more water if the soup is too thick. Season to taste with salt and serve in warm bowls.

Beef and cabbage soup with mustard

The spices and fresh herbs in this soup add a twist to a traditional combination. If you are using dried herbs, the general rule is that you should add half the quantity of fresh herbs given here.

15

PREP

75

COOK

6

SERVES

filling

1 Heat the oil in a large, heavy saucepan, add the beef, and cook over a moderate to high heat for 2 minutes, turning each piece once. Add the onions and cook, stirring frequently, for 3 minutes.

2 Add the stock, caraway seeds, marjoram, and thyme to the soup and bring to a boil, then reduce the heat, partially cover, and simmer for 35–40 minutes. Add the potatoes and cabbage, partially cover, and cook for an additional 25 minutes.

3 Using a slotted spoon, transfer the beef to a board. When cool enough to handle, cut into ½ inch dice. Return to the soup. Stir in the mustard and cook for 2 minutes without boiling. Serve immediately in warm bowls.

2 tablespoons **olive oil**

8 oz lean **beef**, in 1–2 pieces

2 **onions**, finely chopped

6 cups **Beef Stock** (see page 18)

2 teaspoons **caraway seeds**

1 teaspoon chopped **marjoram**

½ teaspoon chopped **thyme**

1½ cups diced **potatoes**

1½ cups finely shredded **Savoy cabbage**

1 tablespoon **Dijon mustard**

¼ cup **butter**

1 large **onion**, chopped

15–16 oz can **sauerkraut**, drained and chopped

2 tablespoons **paprika**

1 tablespoon **caraway seeds**

6 cups **Vegetable Stock** (see page 19)

2 tablespoons **tomato paste**

¼ teaspoon **superfine sugar**

3 cups diced **potatoes**

salt

TO GARNISH:

4–6 tablespoons **sour cream**

1–2 tablespoons snipped **chives**

10

PREP

50

COOK

6

SERVES

spicy

Hungarian sauerkraut soup

The unique blend of sweet paprika, tangy sauerkraut, and fragrant caraway seeds gives this soup a distinctive flavor. Use sweet Hungarian paprika if you can find it.

1 Melt the butter in a large, heavy saucepan, add the onion and cook over a moderate heat for about 5 minutes or until the butter has softened but not browned.

2 Add the sauerkraut, paprika, and caraway seeds and cook, stirring constantly, for 2 minutes. Add the stock, tomato paste, sugar, and potatoes. Stir, bring to a boil, and season to taste with salt. Reduce the heat, cover, and simmer for about 45 minutes.

3 In a small bowl, mix the sour cream with the chives. Spoon the soup into warm bowls, garnish each portion with 1 tablespoon of the sour cream mixture and serve immediately.

White cabbage soup with meatballs

Cabbage, in all its varieties, is a favorite ingredient in European peasant soups. In this delicious, hearty dish, the smooth, hard-packed white cabbage, also known as Dutch cabbage, is the chief component.

1 Discard the outer leaves and core of the cabbage. Shred the cabbage leaves roughly.

2 Melt the butter in a large, heavy saucepan, add the cabbage and sugar and cook, stirring constantly, until the cabbage is golden. Add the stock, allspice berries, and peppercorns, cover and simmer for 30–35 minutes or until the cabbage is tender. Add salt to taste.

3 Make the meatballs. Put the bread crumbs in a bowl, add the measured water and allow to soak for 3 minutes. Add all the remaining ingredients and stir the mixture vigorously with a fork until smooth. Shape the mixture into balls the size of walnuts.

4 Bring the soup to a boil. Drop in the meatballs one by one. Reduce the heat and simmer for 10 minutes. Transfer to a warm tureen and serve in large, warm soup bowls.

25

PREP

50

COOK

4

SERVES

hearty

1 **white cabbage**, about 1¾ lb

¼ cup **butter**

2 teaspoons **superfine sugar**

6 cups **Beef Stock** (see page 18)

3 **allspice berries**

6 **white peppercorns**

salt

MEATBALLS:

2 tablespoons **dried white bread crumbs**

⅔ cup **water**

8 oz **lean ground veal**

8 oz **lean ground pork**

2 **egg yolks**

1 teaspoon **salt**

¼ teaspoon **white pepper**

1 teaspoon **Worcestershire sauce**

1 teaspoon **Dijon mustard**

Oxtail soup

¼ cup **butter**, **lard**, or **drippings**

1 **oxtail**, about 2 lb, cut into 2 inch pieces, excess fat removed

1½ cups chopped **onions**

3 **celery sticks**, chopped

1⅔ cups chopped **carrots**

1 **bay leaf**, crushed

6 **black peppercorns**, crushed

2 **cloves**

¼ teaspoon **superfine sugar**

3 quarts **water**

1 tablespoon **all-purpose flour**

milk, for mixing

⅔ cup **red wine** or 2 tablespoons **dry sherry**

salt and **pepper**

finely chopped **parsley**, to garnish

20

PREP

255

COOK

6

SERVES

classic

This classic soup has stood the test of time, remaining a firm favorite today. Containing peppercorns, bay, and cloves, it's packed full of wonderful flavors, the lengthy cooking time allowing these to develop to the full.

1 Melt the butter, lard, or drippings in a large, heavy saucepan, add the oxtail and onions, and cook over a moderate heat, turning the oxtail once, until just browned.

2 Add the celery, carrots, bay leaf, peppercorns, cloves, and sugar. Season to taste with salt and pepper. Pour in the measured water and bring to a boil. Reduce the heat, cover, and simmer for about 4 hours or until the oxtail is tender.

3 Take the oxtail pieces from the pan, strip the meat from the bones, shred and return the meat to the pan. Discard the bones.

4 In a small bowl, mix the flour with enough milk to make a thin paste. Beat it into the soup, stirring until the soup thickens. Add the wine or sherry and bring the soup slowly to a boil. Serve the soup immediately in warm soup bowls, garnished with finely chopped parsley.

Mulligatawny soup

20
PREP

35
COOK

6
SERVES

spicy

The word mulligatawny is a corruption of the Tamil word **milagu-tuanni**, which roughly means "pepper water." It was introduced to the British Raj by Indian cooks during the 19th century and became known by its present name. The soup should be highly flavored and very spicy.

1 In a blender or food processor, blend the onion, garlic, and ginger with the dry spices to a smooth paste.

2 Heat the oil in a large, heavy saucepan, add the onion paste, and cook over a moderate heat, stirring, for 2–3 minutes. Add the chicken breasts and cook, stirring, for about 1–2 minutes.

3 Slowly add the stock and water, stirring constantly. Add the rice and lentils. Simmer for 15–20 minutes or until the rice is tender.

4 Remove the chicken, cut it into small pieces and set aside. In a blender or food processor, blend 4 cups of the soup until smooth. Return to the pan and stir well. Add a little more water if the soup is too thick.

5 Add the lemon juice, creamed coconut, and reserved chicken. Stir well and reheat gently, without boiling, for 3–5 minutes. Ladle into warm soup bowls, garnish each portion with a lemon slice, and serve immediately.

1 **onion**, chopped

2 **garlic cloves**, chopped

1 inch piece of fresh **gingerroot**, peeled and chopped

1 teaspoon **ground coriander**

¼ teaspoon **cayenne pepper** (or to taste)

½ teaspoon **ground cumin**

1 teaspoon **ground turmeric**

4 teaspoons **vegetable oil**

3 boneless, skinless **chicken breasts**, halved

5 cups **Chicken Stock** (see page 17)

5 cups **water**

¼ cup **white long-grain rice**

½ cup **red lentils**, washed and drained

1 tablespoon **lemon juice**

2 tablespoons grated **creamed coconut**

salt

6 **lemon slices**, to garnish

4 tablespoons **olive oil**

1 **garlic clove**, chopped

1 **onion**, chopped

5 cups **Beef Stock** (see page 18)

3 cups **water**

10 oz lean **pork**, cut into ¾ inch strips

2 **carrots**, chopped

10 oz **Savoy cabbage**, roughly chopped

½ cup **pearl barley**

10 oz **potatoes**, cut into ½ inch cubes

salt and **pepper**

15

PREP

55

COOK

6

SERVES

filling

Barley soup with pork and cabbage

The pearl barley is a lovely complement to the rich pork, and the cabbage adds color to this delicious winter soup. Use any spring cabbage if you cannot find a Savoy.

1 Heat the oil in a large, heavy saucepan, add the garlic and onion and cook over a moderate heat for about 5 minutes or until just softened.

2 Add the stock, measured water, pork, carrots, cabbage, and barley and bring to a boil. Reduce the heat, cover, and simmer for 20 minutes.

3 Add the potatoes and season to taste with salt and pepper. Add a little more water if the soup is too thick. Cover and simmer, stirring occasionally, for an additional 30 minutes. Serve immediately in warm soup bowls.

Goulash soup

15

PREP

75

COOK

Goulash stew and soup originated in Hungary and later became popular dishes in Austria. Although several variations exist, the chief ingredients remain the paprika and caraway seeds that lend the soup its uniquely aromatic flavor.

6

SERVES

1 Heat the oil in a large, heavy saucepan, add the beef, in batches, and cook over a moderate heat until browned. As each batch browns, remove with a slotted spoon and drain on paper towels. Add the onions, garlic, and celery to the pan and cook for 5 minutes or until softened.

spicy

2 Remove from the heat and stir in the paprika, caraway seeds, stock, and measured water. Add the thyme, bay leaves, Tabasco sauce, and tomato paste. Stir well and add the browned beef. Bring to a boil, then reduce the heat, partially cover, and simmer for about 30 minutes.

3 Add the potatoes and carrots and simmer for an additional 30 minutes or until the potatoes are tender. Remove and discard the bay leaves. Spoon the soup into warm soup bowls, garnish each portion with sour cream, if desired, and serve immediately.

3 tablespoons **vegetable oil**

1½ lb boneless lean **beef**, cut into 1 inch strips

2 **onions**, chopped

2 **garlic cloves**, crushed

2 **celery sticks**, sliced

3 tablespoons **paprika**

1 tablespoon **caraway seeds**

5 cups **Beef Stock** (see page 18)

2½ cups **water**

¼ teaspoon **dried thyme**

2 **bay leaves**

¼ teaspoon **Tabasco sauce** (or to taste)

3 tablespoons **tomato paste**

8 oz **potatoes**, cut into ½ inch cubes

3 **carrots**, cut into ½ inch cubes

6–8 teaspoons **sour cream** (optional)

8 oz **pork** tenderloin

7 cups **Chicken Stock**
(see page 17)

3 tablespoons **soy sauce**

2 tablespoons **dry sherry**

2 tablespoons **sesame oil**

2 inch piece of fresh
gingerroot, peeled and
cut into matchsticks

2 **garlic cloves**, crushed

1¼ teaspoons **ground
coriander**

1 teaspoon **ground
turmeric**

¼ teaspoon **chili powder**

4 oz **egg noodles**

4 oz **creamed coconut**,
dissolved in 1¼ cups
boiling water

1 **green bell pepper**,
cored, seeded, and cut
into matchsticks

5 **scallions**, sliced

8 oz **green beans**, halved

2 **carrots**, cut into thin
matchsticks

1¼ cups **bean sprouts**

salt and **pepper**

15

PREP

45

COOK

4

SERVES

feast

Laksa

This soup, originally from Singapore, is a substantial mixture of pork, egg noodles, vegetables, coconut, and spices and could be served as a main course.

1 Put the pork, 6 cups of the stock, the soy sauce, and sherry in a large saucepan and bring to a boil, skimming off the scum that rises to the surface. Reduce the heat, partially cover, and simmer for about 20 minutes or until the pork is just tender.

2 Meanwhile, heat the oil in a separate large saucepan, add the ginger, garlic, and dry spices and cook over a moderate heat, stirring, for 5 minutes. Remove from the heat.

3 Remove the pork from the liquid. Add the noodles and return to a boil. Cover tightly, remove from the heat and allow to stand for 5 minutes. Cut the pork into thin, short strips.

4 Drain the noodles, adding the liquid to the spice mixture. Add the remaining stock and creamed coconut and bring to a boil. Add the vegetables and simmer for 8–10 minutes.

5 Cut the noodles into short pieces. Add to the soup with the pork and bean sprouts. Season to taste, bring to a boil, and cook for 1–2 minutes. Serve in warm soup bowls.

Spicy chili bean soup

This hearty soup is packed full of highly flavored ingredients, including delicious sausages, which add a rich, rounded flavor. Serve with warmed flour tortillas, sliced into thick strips.

1 Heat the oil in a large, heavy saucepan, add the sausage slices and cook over a moderate heat for 5 minutes or until browned. Remove with a slotted spoon and leave to drain on paper towels.

2 Add the onion to the pan and cook for 5 minutes or until softened. Add the chili powder, cumin, and thyme and cook, stirring constantly, for 1 minute. Add the beans, bay leaf, and stock. Bring to a boil, then reduce the heat, cover, and simmer for 1 hour.

3 Add the garlic, bell pepper, and tomatoes, cover and simmer, stirring occasionally, for an additional 1 hour. Add the sausage slices, then season to taste with salt and cook, stirring frequently, for an additional 5 minutes. Serve in warm soup bowls.

15*

PREP

140

COOK

4

SERVES

hearty

2 tablespoons **olive oil**

4 small or 2 large **Kabanos sausages**, thinly sliced

1 **onion**, chopped

1 tablespoon mild **chili powder** (or to taste)

1 teaspoon **ground cumin**

¼ teaspoon **dried thyme**

1¼ cups **pinto beans**, soaked overnight in cold water, rinsed, and drained

1 **bay leaf**

5 cups **Chicken Stock** (see page 17)

2 **garlic cloves**, crushed

1 large **red bell pepper**, cored, seeded, and chopped

13 oz can chopped **tomatoes**

salt

* Plus overnight soaking

Pot-au-feu

2 lb **beef** shank with bones, excess fat removed

1 teaspoon **salt**

1 **bouquet garni**

6 **black peppercorns**, crushed

1 unpeeled **onion**, studded with 4 **cloves**

1 **garlic clove**, crushed

3 **carrots**, chopped

2 **celery sticks**, sliced

3 **leeks**, sliced

1 lb **potatoes**, diced

3 tablespoons finely chopped **parsley**, to garnish

15

PREP

220

COOK

4

SERVES

classic

Pot-au-feu is often referred to as the national soup of France. Although the French treat it as a main course and usually serve the meat separately, there are no firm rules when it comes to preparing this substantial dish, and in this recipe it is more of a soup than a main course.

1 Put the beef and bones in a large saucepan and add cold water to cover. Add the salt and bring to a boil, skimming off the scum that rises to the surface.

2 Reduce the heat and add the bouquet garni, peppercorns, studded onion, and the garlic. Partially cover and simmer for about 2½ hours or until the meat is almost tender. Skim from time to time if necessary. Check occasionally if the water level in the saucepan falls and add more water.

3 Remove and discard the bones, bouquet garni, and studded onion. Add the vegetables and simmer for an additional 1 hour or until all the vegetables are tender. Remove the beef, cut it into pieces, then return to the soup and simmer until heated through. Serve the soup in large, warm soup plates, garnished with the parsley.

Game broth

15

PREP

135

COOK

6

SERVES

posh

Game includes partridge, wood pigeon, and pheasant. Because the season is relatively short, it's not always easy to get fresh game, but you can use frozen meat instead. Remember to allow plenty of time for defrosting before you need it.

1 Melt the butter in a large, heavy saucepan, add the game trimmings or leftovers, setting the breast of game aside, with the beef, ham, onion, celery, and carrot. Cook over a moderate heat, stirring frequently, for about 8 minutes or until the vegetables just begin to brown.

2 Add the stock, bouquet garni, bay leaf, juniper berries, peppercorns, and parsley to the pan. Bring to a boil, then reduce the heat, partially cover, and simmer for about 2 hours. Add more water if the liquid reduces too much.

3 Strain the liquid through a fine sieve into a clean saucepan. Discard the solids in the sieve. Stir the sherry into the broth and season to taste with salt. Add the reserved breast of game and simmer until heated through. Serve the broth in warm soup bowls.

¼ cup **butter**

1 lb cooked **game**, trimmings, or leftovers, plus 8 oz cooked **breast of game**, cut into thin strips

8 oz lean **beef**, thinly cut across the grain

2 oz lean cooked **ham**, finely chopped

1 **onion**, chopped

1 **celery stick**, sliced

1 **carrot**, chopped

8 cups **Beef Stock** (see page 18)

1 **bouquet garni**

1 **bay leaf**

3 **juniper berries**

6 **black peppercorns**

2 sprigs of **parsley**

2 tablespoons **dry sherry**

salt

Avgolemono

10

PREP

50

COOK

4

SERVES

light

2 **chicken quarters**, each about 12 oz

2 **carrots**, chopped

1 small **onion**, sliced

1 **celery stick**

2 **bay leaves**

6 **white peppercorns**

5 cups **water**

¼ cup **white long-grain rice**

2 **egg yolks**

3 tablespoons **lemon juice**

4 tablespoons chopped **parsley**

salt and **pepper**

This lemon, chicken, and egg soup is made throughout Greece. The eggs thicken the soup as it is heated, but you must be careful not to boil the soup because otherwise the eggs will curdle.

1 Put the chicken, carrots, onion, celery, bay leaves, peppercorns, and measured water into a large, heavy saucepan. Bring slowly to a boil, skimming the scum that rises to the surface, then reduce the heat and simmer gently for 30 minutes.

2 Strain the stock into a clean saucepan. Cut the chicken into bite-size pieces and set aside. Add the rice to the stock and simmer for 15 minutes or until tender.

3 In a small bowl, beat together the egg yolks, lemon juice, and 2 tablespoons of the stock, then gradually beat the mixture into the stock in the pan. Add the reserved chicken and parsley. Season to taste with salt and pepper. Reheat gently without boiling and serve hot in warm soup bowls.

Chicken and corn soup

This soup originally came from southern China, but it is extremely popular in the West. The creamed-style corn and canned corn kernels give it texture, and it is thickened with a minimum of cornstarch.

1 Put the 6 cups stock in a large, heavy saucepan and bring to a boil. Add the creamed-style corn and corn kernels, then reduce the heat and simmer for 5 minutes.

2 Add the chicken to the pan, then return the soup to a boil. Add the pepper. Blend the cornstarch with the 2 tablespoons stock, slowly stir into the soup and simmer until slightly thickened. Remove from the heat.

3 Slowly drizzle in the beaten eggs, stirring constantly, ideally with chopsticks (the stirring helps to form the egg into fine threads). Serve immediately in warm soup bowls.

10

PREP

20

COOK

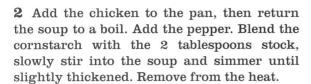

4

SERVES

quick

6 cups **Chicken Stock** (see page 17), plus 2 tablespoons

9 oz can creamed-style **corn**

9 oz can **corn kernels**, drained

4 oz cooked **chicken**, finely shredded

½ teaspoon **white pepper**

2 teaspoons **cornstarch**

2 **eggs**, beaten

2 tablespoons extra virgin **olive oil**

1 **onion**, finely chopped

1 **garlic clove**, finely chopped

⅔ cup **dry white wine**

2½ cups **Chicken Stock** (see page 17)

4 boneless, skinless **chicken breasts**, each about 7 oz

1⅓ cups **fava beans**, thawed if frozen

2 cups **peas**, thawed if frozen

4 tablespoons chopped **chives**, **mint**, **oregano**, or **parsley**

salt and **pepper**

15

PREP

16

COOK

4

SERVES

simple

Chicken with vegetable broth

This recipe really needs a good-quality stock. If you do not have time to make your own, look out for fresh stocks in the chiller section of large supermarkets.

1 Heat the oil in a large, nonstick skillet, add the onion and garlic and cook over a moderate heat for 5 minutes. Add the wine and boil to reduce by half. Add the stock and chicken and bring to a gentle simmer. Cover and cook for 8 minutes. Remove the chicken from the pan, wrap it in foil and keep warm.

2 Add the beans and peas to the stock and cook for 2–3 minutes or until tender. Add the herbs and salt and pepper to taste.

3 Spoon the vegetables and broth into 4 large, warm soup bowls. Slice the chicken and arrange in the bowls. Serve immediately.

Turkey and vegetable soup

This soup proves that turkey shouldn't be eaten just at Thanksgiving! The drumstick contains both white and dark meat, so it will add depth of flavor to the finished dish.

25
PREP

120
COOK

8
SERVES

feast

1 Put the drumstick in a large, heavy saucepan. Add the measured water, studded onion, parsley sprigs, bouquet garni, salt, thyme, and marjoram and bring to a boil. Reduce the heat, partially cover, and simmer for 45 minutes.

2 Add the chopped onion, carrots, and celery and simmer over a low to moderate heat for 30 minutes, then add the lentils, potatoes, leeks, and turnips. Simmer until all the vegetables are tender. Remove the drumstick and allow to cool. Remove and discard the bouquet garni, studded onion and parsley, thyme and marjoram stalks.

3 Cut the turkey meat off the bone, and remove and discard the skin. Carefully remove and discard any small bones. Cut the meat into small pieces and return to the pan. Add the soy sauce and season to taste with pepper. Reheat thoroughly and serve in a warm soup tureen, garnished with parsley.

1 large **turkey drumstick**, about 1½ lb

2½ quarts **water**

1 small unpeeled **onion**, studded with 4 **cloves**, plus 1 large **onion**, peeled and chopped

2 sprigs of **parsley**

1 **bouquet garni**

1 teaspoon **salt**

1 sprig of **thyme**

1 sprig of **marjoram**

3 **carrots**, chopped

2 **celery sticks**, sliced

1 cup **red lentils**, washed and drained

8 oz **potatoes**, cut into ½ inch cubes

3 **leeks**, sliced

3 **turnips**, cut into ½ inch cubes

2 tablespoons **light soy sauce**

pepper

3–4 tablespoons finely chopped **parsley**, to garnish

fish and shellfish

Mussel soup

2 tablespoons **olive oil**

2 **onions**, chopped

2 **garlic cloves**, crushed

1 **red chili**, chopped

5 oz piece of **bacon**, chopped

2 lb **mussels**, scrubbed and debearded

2 x 13 oz cans chopped **tomatoes**

1½ cups **dry white wine**

good pinch of **saffron threads**

handful of **flat leaf parsley**, roughly chopped

salt and **pepper**

20

PREP

10

COOK

4

SERVES

tasty

It is very important to clean the live mussels thoroughly before using to get rid of any debris. The beards can be pulled off with a sharp tug. Bacon, garlic, chili, and wine are ideal flavorings for the shellfish.

1 Heat the oil in a large, heavy saucepan, add the onions, garlic, chili, and bacon and cook over a moderate heat for 5 minutes.

2 Discard any mussels that are broken or open, or that do not close when tapped on a work surface.

3 Add the mussels, tomatoes, wine, and saffron to the pan, mix well and season to taste with salt and pepper. Cover tightly and simmer for 5 minutes or until all the mussel shells have opened. Discard any mussels that have not opened. Add the parsley and stir well. Serve the soup immediately in warm soup bowls.

Mussel chowder

Use small, plump mussels for this smooth, creamy soup. The large New Zealand mussels are not suitable.

15
PREP

30
COOK

4
SERVES

rich

1 Heat the oil in a large, heavy saucepan, add the bacon, and cook over a moderate heat until browned. Add the onions, celery, and bell pepper and cook for about 5 minutes until just softened.

2 Stir in the stock, potatoes, bay leaf, and marjoram and bring to a boil. Reduce the heat, cover, and simmer for 15–20 minutes or until the potatoes are tender.

3 In a small bowl, blend the flour with ⅔ cup of the milk. Beat the mixture into the chowder and stir until it begins to boil, then slowly add the remaining milk. Season to taste with salt and pepper.

4 Reduce the heat, add the mussels, and simmer gently, stirring occasionally, for 5 minutes, without boiling. Stir in the cream, then pour the chowder into a warm soup tureen. Sprinkle with the parsley to garnish and serve with crusty French bread.

2 tablespoons **olive oil**

8 oz rindless **bacon**, chopped

2 **onions**, finely chopped

1 **celery stick**, thinly sliced

1 **green bell pepper**, cored, seeded, and finely chopped

2 cups **Fish Stock** (see page 16)

2 cups diced **potatoes**

1 **bay leaf**

½ teaspoon chopped **marjoram**

3 tablespoons **all-purpose flour**

1¼ cups **milk**

1 lb cooked shelled **mussels**, thawed if frozen

⅔ cup **light cream**

salt and **white pepper**

1 tablespoon finely chopped **parsley**, to garnish

crusty **French bread**, to serve

1½ lb **baby clams** or **cockles**, cleaned

3 tablespoons **olive oil**, plus extra to serve

2 large **garlic cloves**, 1 finely chopped and 1 bruised

1½ lb **zucchini**, thickly sliced

finely grated zest and juice of 1 **lemon**

1 tablespoon chopped **marjoram**

about 4 cups **Vegetable Stock** (see page 19) or **water**

4 thick slices of country **bread**, toasted

salt and **pepper**

15

PREP

25

COOK

4

SERVES

fresh

Clam and zucchini soup

In Italy, this light, fresh soup of zucchini and clams is called **aquacotta**, which means "cooked water." It is a simple soup, made more substantial by ladling it over toasted bread, as they do in the country.

1 Bring ½ inch water to a boil in a saucepan. Add the clams, cover, and steam until they open. Reserve the juice and remove half of the clams from their shells, keeping the remaining clams in their shells. Discard any clams that have not opened.

2 Heat the oil in a large, heavy saucepan, add the chopped garlic and cook over a low to moderate heat until golden but not browned. Add the zucchini, lemon zest, and marjoram and turn in the oil and garlic. Pour in the stock or water, season lightly with salt and pepper, and bring to simmering point. Cover and simmer for 10 minutes or until the zucchini are tender.

3 Pass the soup through a coarse food mill and return to the pan. Add the reserved clam juice, shelled clams, and lemon juice. Stir in the clams in their shells and heat through.

4 Rub the toasted bread with the bruised garlic clove and place a slice in each soup bowl. Ladle the soup over the bread, drizzle with olive oil, and serve immediately.

Clam chowder

20

PREP

35

COOK

Two pounds of clams provide surprisingly little meat, but the pronounced flavor, combined with the salt pork, makes a rich, hearty soup that's good as an appetizer or, in larger portions, as a main course.

4

SERVES

posh

1 Bring ⅔ cup water to a boil in a saucepan. Add the clams, cover with a tight-fitting lid and cook for 4–5 minutes or until the shells have opened. Drain, reserving the cooking juices, and discard any clams that remain closed. Remove the flesh from the shells and chop it into small pieces.

2 Put the pork and onion in a large saucepan with some of the butter and fry gently for 10 minutes or until browned. Stir in the remaining butter until melted. Add the flour and cook, stirring, for 1 minute.

3 Add the clam cooking juices and 2 cups water, the tomatoes, potatoes, and bay leaves. Bring just to a boil, then reduce the heat, cover, and cook very gently for 15 minutes or until the potatoes are tender.

4 Stir in the clams and parsley and cook very gently for 2 minutes. Add the Tabasco sauce and cream, heat through, and serve.

2 lb **clams**, cleaned

7 oz **salt pork**, finely chopped

1 large **onion**, chopped

1 tablespoon **butter**

1 tablespoon **all-purpose flour**

4 **tomatoes**, skinned and chopped

3 cups diced **potatoes**

2 **bay leaves**

3 tablespoons chopped **parsley**

2 teaspoons **Tabasco sauce**

⅔ cup **light cream**

2 tablespoons **olive oil**

2 **onions**, chopped

2 **celery sticks**, sliced

4 cups **Fish Stock** (see page 16)

12 oz **potatoes**, cut into small cubes

1¾ cups frozen **corn kernels**

5 oz frozen cooked peeled **shrimp**

1 tablespoon chopped **thyme**, **parsley**, or fresh **cilantro** (optional)

salt and **pepper**

crusty **bread**, to serve

10

PREP

25

COOK

4

SERVES

easy

Corn and shrimp chowder

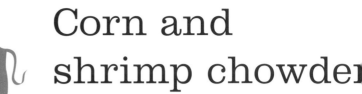

The three main ingredients in this dish—corn, frozen shrimp, and potatoes—are found in most kitchens' emergency reserves. Frozen corn kernels are preferable to canned corn kernels, which have a salty, preserved taste.

1 Heat the oil in a large, heavy saucepan, add the onions and celery and cook over a moderate heat for 5 minutes.

2 Add the stock and bring to a boil. Reduce the heat and add the potatoes. Cover and simmer gently for 8–10 minutes.

3 Add the corn kernels and cook for 5 minutes, then add the shrimp and herbs (if using). Cook gently for an additional 2–3 minutes to heat through. Season with salt and pepper and ladle into warm soup bowls.

Shrimp soup with okra

Okra is used extensively in Creole cuisine. It looks a little like a small zucchini and adds color and texture to dishes. You should be able to buy it in most large supermarkets.

1 Melt the butter in a large, heavy saucepan and add the onion and celery. Cover and cook over a moderate heat until the onion starts to soften but not brown. Add the stock and rice, cover, and cook over a low heat for 20 minutes or until the rice is tender.

2 Prepare the okra by cutting away the conical cap from the stalk end, then cutting the okra into ½ inch slices.

3 Add the okra, tomatoes, shrimp, and ham to the soup and cook, stirring frequently, for an additional 5–8 minutes. Spoon the soup into warm soup bowls and garnish generously with small parsley leaves.

15

PREP

35

COOK

4

SERVES

exotic

¼ cup **butter**

1 **onion**, finely chopped

2 cups thinly sliced **celery sticks**

4 cups **Fish Stock** (see page 16)

¼ cup **white long-grain rice**

8 oz **okra**

2 **tomatoes**, skinned and finely chopped

8 oz cooked peeled **shrimp**, thawed if frozen

2 oz cooked **ham**, cut into fine strips

small **parsley leaves**, to garnish

¼ cup **butter**

2 **garlic cloves**, crushed

1 **onion**, chopped

1 **red bell pepper**, cored, seeded, and finely chopped

4 ripe **tomatoes**, skinned and chopped

¼ teaspoon **cayenne pepper** (or to taste)

5 cups **Fish Stock** (see page 16)

12 oz **okra,** trimmed and sliced

12 oz cooked peeled **shrimp**, thawed if frozen

⅓ cup cooked **white long-grain rice**

1 tablespoon **lime juice**

salt and **pepper**

20

PREP

40

COOK

4

SERVES

spicy

Shrimp gumbo

This Cajun gumbo is a traditional dish along the Louisiana coast. Gumbo can be made with a variety of vegetables, meats, and seafood, but okra is the most important ingredient. The soup can be made 24 hours in advance and kept, covered, in the refrigerator.

1 Melt the butter in a large heavy saucepan, add the garlic and onion and cook over a moderate heat for 5 minutes or until softened.

2 Add the bell pepper to the pan and cook for 5 minutes. Stir in the tomatoes and cayenne pepper and mix well. Pour in the stock and bring to a boil. Stir in the okra. Reduce the heat, cover, and cook, stirring occasionally, for 20 minutes.

3 Add the shrimp, rice, and lime juice to the soup, then stir well. Cover and simmer for an additional 5–8 minutes. Season to taste with salt and pepper and add a little more cayenne pepper, if desired. Serve immediately in warm soup bowls.

Simple shrimp bisque

15

PREP

40

COOK

6

SERVES

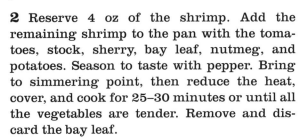

simple

This recipe really is as simple as its name suggests. You can buy ready peeled shrimp or, if you have the time and inclination, buy them whole and peel them yourself.

1 Melt the butter in a large, heavy saucepan, add the onion, carrot, and celery and cook over a moderate heat for 5 minutes or until just softened.

2 Reserve 4 oz of the shrimp. Add the remaining shrimp to the pan with the tomatoes, stock, sherry, bay leaf, nutmeg, and potatoes. Season to taste with pepper. Bring to simmering point, then reduce the heat, cover, and cook for 25–30 minutes or until all the vegetables are tender. Remove and discard the bay leaf.

3 In a blender or food processor, blend the soup in batches, and transfer it to a clean saucepan. Add the reserved shrimp, season to taste with salt, and reheat gently. Just before serving, stir in the cream and sprinkle with the parsley or chives to garnish.

¼ cup **butter**

1 small **onion**, finely chopped

1 **carrot**, finely chopped

1 **celery stick**, thinly sliced

1 lb cooked peeled **shrimp**, thawed if frozen

13 oz can chopped **tomatoes**

4 cups **Fish Stock** (see page 16)

1 tablespoon **medium dry sherry**

1 **bay leaf**

pinch of **grated nutmeg**

2 cups thinly sliced **potatoes**

¼ cup **heavy cream**

salt and **pepper**

1 tablespoon finely chopped **parsley** or snipped **chives**, to garnish

¼ cup **butter**

2 **fennel bulbs**, trimmed and finely sliced, fronds reserved to garnish

2½ cups **Fish Stock** (see page 16)

2½ cups **milk**

¼ teaspoon **white pepper**

2½ cups diced **potatoes**

6 oz cooked peeled **shrimp**, thawed if frozen

⅔ cup **light cream**

salt

PREP

COOK

SERVES

stylish

Shrimp and fennel soup

This soup doesn't need many ingredients because shrimp and fennel are such wonderfully unique flavors that can hold their own. The subtle aniseed taste of fennel is mellowed by the addition of milk and cream.

1 Melt the butter in a large, heavy saucepan and add the sliced fennel. Cover tightly and cook over a moderate heat, stirring occasionally, for 5 minutes or until just beginning to soften.

2 Add the stock, milk, pepper, and potatoes and bring to simmering point. Reduce the heat, cover, and simmer gently for 15–20 minutes or until the vegetables are tender.

3 In a blender or food processor, blend the soup in batches, then transfer it to a clean saucepan. Add the shrimp, season to taste with salt, and stir in the cream. Reheat gently without boiling. Spoon into warm soup bowls and garnish with a sprinkling of finely chopped fennel fronds.

Cream of celery and shrimp soup

This wonderfully creamy soup can be served chilled. It would make a great dinner party appetizer because you can prepare the whole dish in advance and leave it chilling in the refrigerator until you are ready to serve.

1 Mix together the soup and milk in a large, heavy saucepan. Add the paprika and pepper. Bring to simmering point and cook, stirring constantly, for 5 minutes. Remove from heat.

2 If serving the soup hot, stir in the yogurt and shrimp and gently heat through for about 2 minutes without boiling. Spoon into warm soup bowls, garnish each portion with snipped chives, and serve immediately.

3 If serving the soup chilled, pour the soup into a bowl and allow to cool. Stir in the yogurt and shrimp, cover, and chill in a refrigerator for at least 3 hours. Serve the soup in chilled bowls, each portion garnished with snipped chives.

5*
PREP

10
COOK

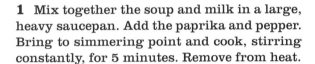
3
SERVES

quick

10 oz can **condensed cream of celery soup**

1¼ cups **milk**

1 teaspoon **paprika**

½ teaspoon **white pepper**

2 tablespoons **plain yogurt**

5 oz cooked peeled **shrimp**, thawed if frozen

snipped **chives**, to garnish

* Plus 3 hours chilling if served cold

fish and shellfish 59

5 **red bird's eye chilies**

6 **kaffir lime leaves**

1 string of **green peppercorns**

1 **lemon grass stalk**, finely sliced

4 cups **water**

2 tablespoons **Thai fish sauce**

2 teaspoons **superfine sugar**

1 lb raw peeled and deveined **jumbo shrimp**

4 tablespoons **kaffir lime juice**

handful of fresh **cilantro**

plain boiled rice, to serve

10

PREP

15

COOK

4

SERVES

exotic

Shrimp and kaffir lime soup

Strings of green peppercorns can be found in specialty Asian stores. They are added to Thai and Cambodian curries to add a peppery flavor, but are not eaten. If you cannot find them, use peppercorns in brine and tie 1 tablespoon of the drained peppercorns in a piece of cheesecloth. Discard before eating.

1 Put the chilies, kaffir lime leaves, peppercorns, lemon grass, and measured water in a large, heavy saucepan and slowly bring to a boil. Boil for 10 minutes.

2 Reduce the heat and add the fish sauce and sugar. When the liquid is simmering, add the shrimp and simmer gently for 2–3 minutes or until they have turned pink. Remove the pan from the heat and add the lime juice and cilantro. Serve immediately in warm bowls with plain boiled rice.

Crab and rice soup

Crab has a wonderfully rich, distinctive taste that takes well to other flavors, such as saffron. Although real saffron is expensive, you only need a couple of threads to make a big difference to the flavor and color of a dish.

1 Heat the oil in a large, heavy saucepan, add the crab meat and cook over a moderate heat, stirring frequently, until lightly browned. Add the onion and cook, stirring constantly, for 5 minutes. Add the tomatoes, paprika, salt, and measured boiling water. Cover and simmer gently for 45 minutes.

2 Meanwhile, pound the garlic with a pinch of salt and the parsley sprigs in a mortar with a pestle. Add the saffron and 2 tablespoons of the simmering stock. Stir well.

3 Add the rice and the garlic mixture to the pan. Partially cover and simmer for 20 minutes or until the rice is tender. Remove the pan from the heat and allow the soup to rest for 2–3 minutes. Stir, then taste and adjust the seasoning if necessary. Pour the soup into a warm tureen and serve hot with croutons, if desired.

15
PREP

80
COOK

6
SERVES

posh

4 tablespoons **olive oil**

1 lb **white crab meat**, cut into ½ inch pieces

1 **onion**, chopped

¾ cup skinned and chopped **tomatoes**

1 teaspoon **paprika**

½ teaspoon **salt** (or to taste)

7 cups boiling **water**

2 **garlic cloves**

2 sprigs of **parsley**, leaves stripped from the stalks

2 **saffron threads**

1 cup **white long-grain rice**

croutons, to garnish (optional)

10 oz can **condensed cream of tomato soup**

1¼ cups **milk**

6 oz can **white crab meat** in brine

½ teaspoon **mild curry powder**

1 teaspoon **Worcestershire sauce**

2 teaspoons **medium dry sherry**

2 tablespoons **heavy cream**

snipped **chives** or finely chopped **parsley**, to garnish (optional)

croutons, to serve (optional)

5

PREP

10

COOK

4

SERVES

easy

Crab meat bisque

This is such a quick and easy soup that you can make it for lunch or dinner even if you are short of time. Make sure you have all the ingredients ready before you begin cooking.

1 Mix the soup and milk in a large, heavy saucepan. Bring to simmering point and cook, stirring constantly, for 3 minutes. Add the crab meat with the brine, then stir in the curry powder, Worcestershire sauce, and sherry. Cook, stirring, for an additional 3 minutes or until almost boiling.

2 Remove the pan from the heat and stir in the cream. Spoon the soup into warm soup bowls, garnish each portion with snipped chives or finely chopped parsley, if desired, and serve immediately. Serve with croutons if the bisque is intended to be more substantial.

Corn soup with crab meat

PREP 15

COOK 20

SERVES 4

light

Ginger works well with the Asian theme of this recipe. To prepare, simply cut a large piece and carefully slice off the skin. Use a cheese grater to grate the required amount, turning the piece of ginger as you grate so that it doesn't become stringy.

1 In a small bowl, beat the egg white with the oil. Set aside. In a separate small bowl, blend the cornstarch with the measured water. Set aside.

2 Bring the stock to a boil in a large, heavy saucepan. Add the corn kernels, reduce the heat, and simmer for 10 minutes. Then add the sherry, ginger, salt, and sugar. Stir in the reserved cornstarch mixture. Bring to a boil, stirring, then reduce the heat and simmer, stirring frequently, for 3–5 minutes.

3 Add the crab meat to the pan and stir well. Cook for 2 minutes. Pour in the reserved egg white mixture slowly and in a steady stream, stirring constantly. Ladle the soup into a warm tureen, sprinkle with the scallion tops to garnish, and serve immediately.

1 **egg white**

1 teaspoon **sesame oil**

2 teaspoons **cornstarch**

2 teaspoons **water**

5 cups **Chicken Stock** (see page 17)

9 oz can **corn kernels**, drained

2 tablespoons **dry sherry**

2 teaspoons grated fresh **gingerroot**

½ teaspoon **salt**

1 teaspoon **superfine sugar**

6 oz can **white crab meat** in brine, drained

2 tablespoons finely chopped **scallion tops**, to garnish

2 tablespoons **butter**

1 tablespoon **sunflower oil**

1 **onion**, chopped

1 **baking potato**, diced

2½ cups lowfat **milk**

1 **fish bouillon cube**, crumbled

2 **bay leaves**

grated **nutmeg**

1 fillet of undyed **smoked haddock**, about 8 oz, cut in half

2½ cups **baby spinach**, stalks discarded, torn into pieces

salt and **pepper**

4 broiled slices of **bacon**, to garnish (optional)

15

PREP

25

COOK

3

SERVES

filling

Haddock and spinach chowder

American-style chowders feature among the easiest soups to prepare because the fish and vegetables are simply poached in milk and left in their chunky form, resulting in a creamy, satisfying soup.

1 Melt the butter with the oil in a large, heavy saucepan, add the onion, and cook over a moderate heat for 5 minutes or until softened but not browned. Add the potato and cook, stirring frequently, for about 5 minutes or until lightly browned.

2 Stir in the milk, bouillon cube, bay leaves, and nutmeg. Season to taste with salt and pepper. Add the haddock and bring to a boil. Reduce the heat, cover, and simmer for 10 minutes or until the haddock flakes easily. Using a slotted spoon, transfer the haddock to a plate and allow to cool. Remove and discard the skin and flake the flesh into pieces, carefully removing and discarding any remaining bones.

3 Add the spinach to the pan and cook for 2–3 minutes or until tender. Add the haddock and reheat gently.

4 Cut the broiled bacon into strips (if using). Ladle the soup into warm soup bowls and garnish with the bacon.

Haddock and corn chowder

15 PREP

Smoked haddock has real depth of flavor, and it combines here to perfect effect with corn kernels and milk to produce a rich, thick soup that's delicious served with fresh crusty bread.

25 COOK

1 Put the potato and bay leaf in a large, heavy saucepan. Add the milk and measured water and bring to a boil. Reduce the heat and simmer for 5 minutes or until the potato is almost tender.

2 Add the haddock, cover, and simmer for 10 minutes. Add the corn kernels and peas and simmer for an additional 5 minutes. Remove and discard the bay leaf.

3 In a small bowl, blend the cornstarch, paprika, and pepper with 3–4 tablespoons of the soup liquid. Add the cornstarch mixture to the pan and cook, stirring constantly, for 5 minutes or until the soup has thickened. Taste and add salt if necessary, then stir in the parsley. Serve the soup immediately in warm soup bowls.

4 SERVES

rich

1 large **potato**, diced

1 **bay leaf**

1¼ cups **milk**

2½ cups **water**

8–10 oz skinned **smoked haddock** fillet, roughly chopped, with any remaining bones removed

7 oz can **corn kernels**, drained

3 tablespoons frozen **peas**

1½ tablespoons **cornstarch**

¼ teaspoon **paprika**

½ teaspoon **white pepper**

salt (optional)

2 tablespoons finely chopped **parsley**

2 tablespoons **butter**

8 oz **fennel bulbs**, trimmed and finely sliced, fronds reserved to garnish

1 **leek**, white part only, sliced

2½ cups **Fish Stock** (see page 16)

1 **bay leaf**

2½ cups thinly sliced **potatoes**

8 oz skinned **haddock** fillet

1¼ cups **milk**

½ teaspoon **white pepper**

salt

15

PREP

30

COOK

4

SERVES

tasty

Haddock and fennel soup

The slight aniseed flavor of fennel enhances most fish soups. Its feathery fronds can be finely chopped and sprinkled over the soup as a garnish.

1 Melt the butter in a large, heavy saucepan, add the sliced fennel and leek and cook for 5 minutes or until softened. Add the stock, bay leaf, and potatoes and bring to a boil. Reduce the heat, cover, and simmer for 10–15 minutes or until all the vegetables are tender. Remove and discard the bay leaf.

2 Meanwhile, in a separate saucepan, mix together the haddock, milk, and pepper and bring to a boil. Reduce the heat, cover, and simmer for 5 minutes. Remove the pan from the heat and allow to stand, covered, for 5 minutes. Break the fish into large flakes.

3 In a blender or food processor, blend 1¼ cups of the vegetable and stock mixture until smooth. Return to the pan and add the haddock and milk mixture. Stir well and heat through without boiling. Serve the soup in warm soup bowls, garnished with finely chopped fennel fronds.

Smoked haddock and corn soup

Wild rice isn't actually rice; it's a grain that's grown in marshes. It adds an unusual nutty taste that is complemented by the saltiness of the smoked haddock.

15
PREP

90
COOK

4
SERVES

thick

⅓ cup **wild rice**

8 oz **smoked haddock**

2½ cups **milk**

1 **bay leaf**

¼ cup **butter**

1 large **onion**, chopped

1 **leek**, trimmed, cleaned, and sliced

1 **celery stick**, chopped

1 **garlic clove**, crushed

1 tablespoon **thyme** leaves

4 cups **Chicken Stock** (see page 17)

pinch of **grated nutmeg**

¾ cup **corn kernels**, thawed if frozen

salt and **pepper**

2 tablespoons chopped **parsley**, to garnish

1 Put the rice in a saucepan and cover with water. Bring to a boil. Reduce the heat and simmer for 40–45 minutes until tender. Drain.

2 Put the haddock, milk, and bay leaf in a large, heavy saucepan and bring to a boil. Reduce the heat and simmer for 8–10 minutes until just cooked. Using a slotted spoon, transfer the haddock to a plate and allow to cool. Remove and discard the skin and flake the flesh into pieces, carefully removing and discarding any bones. Strain the milk through a sieve and reserve.

3 Melt the butter in a clean, large, heavy saucepan, add the onion, leek, celery, and garlic and cook over a low heat, stirring frequently, for 8–10 minutes until softened but not browned. Add the thyme, stock, reserved milk, nutmeg, and salt and pepper to taste. Bring to a boil. Reduce the heat and simmer for 10 minutes. Add the corn and simmer for 5 minutes. Add the rice and haddock and simmer for 5 minutes. Serve in warm soup bowls, sprinkled with the parsley.

¼ cup **butter**

2 cups thinly sliced **celery sticks**, leaves reserved to garnish

1 **leek**, white part only, sliced

2½ cups **Fish Stock** (see page 16)

1 **bay leaf**

2½ cups thinly sliced **potatoes**

8 oz skinned **cod** fillet

1¼ cups **milk**

½ teaspoon **white pepper**

salt

15

PREP

30

COOK

4

SERVES

simple

Cod and celery soup

This variation on Haddock and Fennel Soup (see page 66) is an ideal alternative for people who do not like the aniseed taste of fennel.

1 Melt the butter in a large, heavy saucepan, add the celery and leek and cook for 5 minutes or until softened. Add the stock, bay leaf, and potatoes and bring to a boil. Reduce the heat, cover, and simmer for 10–15 minutes or until all the vegetables are tender. Remove and discard the bay leaf.

2 Meanwhile, in a separate saucepan, mix together the cod, milk, and pepper and bring to a boil. Reduce the heat, cover, and simmer for 5 minutes. Remove from the heat and allow to stand, covered, for 5 minutes. Break the fish into large flakes.

3 In a blender or food processor, blend 1¼ cups of the vegetable and stock mixture until smooth. Return to the pan and add the cod and milk mixture. Stir well and heat through without boiling. Serve the soup in warm soup bowls, garnished with finely chopped celery leaves.

Cod soup with rice and tomatoes

Although you probably wouldn't want to eat a fish head, they are fantastic for adding flavor to soups and fish stock. In this recipe, it will help to enhance the taste of the cod.

20

PREP

90

COOK

4

SERVES

tasty

1½ lb **cod**, skinned and boned

4 large **tomatoes**, skinned and roughly chopped

2 large **onions**, thinly sliced

2 **celery sticks**, thinly sliced

4 sprigs of **parsley**

1 **fish head**

7 cups **water**

5 tablespoons **olive oil**

¼ cup **white short-grain rice**

salt and **pepper**

1 Rinse the cod under cold running water. Drain well. Cut into 2 inch pieces. Put in a colander, sprinkle with 1 teaspoon salt, and allow to stand.

2 Put all the vegetables, parsley, and fish head in a large, heavy saucepan. Add the measured water and season to taste with salt and pepper. Bring to a boil, then reduce the heat and simmer for 45 minutes. Remove and discard the fish head and parsley.

3 Rinse the cod pieces again under cold running water, add to the pan, and cook over a moderate heat for 15–20 minutes or until cooked but still firm. Using a slotted spoon, transfer the cod pieces to a dish, cover and keep hot. Slowly pour the oil into the soup, then add the rice. Partially cover, and cook over a moderate heat for 25 minutes or until the rice is tender. Return the cod pieces to the soup and gently heat through. Taste and adjust the seasoning if necessary, then serve immediately in warm soup bowls.

Kipper soup

15

PREP

20

COOK

6

SERVES

easy

12 oz **kipper** fillet

2½ cups **water**

2 x 14 oz cans **plum tomatoes**

1 tablespoon **tomato paste**

1½ tablespoons **cornstarch**

1 teaspoon **lemon juice**

1 tablespoon **Worcestershire sauce**

¼ teaspoon **celery salt**

cayenne pepper

TO GARNISH:

3 tablespoons **sour cream** (optional)

2 tablespoons snipped **chives**

Kippers are often eaten only at breakfast, so it's good to see them used in this piquant soup. These cured herrings are a natural partner for tomatoes, and the cayenne pepper and Worcestershire sauce add a bit of a kick.

1 Put the kippers in a large, heavy saucepan and add the measured water. Bring to simmering point, then reduce the heat, cover tightly, and cook for 5 minutes. Drain, reserving 2 cups of the liquid.

2 Remove and discard the skin from the kippers and flake the flesh into pieces. In a blender or food processor, blend the fish with the tomatoes, tomato paste, and 1¼ cups of the reserved liquid. Transfer the mixture to a clean saucepan.

3 In a small bowl, blend the cornstarch with the remaining liquid. Stir the cornstarch mixture into the pan and add the lemon juice, Worcestershire sauce, and celery salt, with cayenne pepper to taste. Simmer, stirring, for 5–8 minutes or until the soup thickens slightly. Spoon into warm soup bowls, garnish each portion with a swirl of sour cream, if desired, and a generous sprinkling of snipped chives and serve immediately.

Tuna and red pepper chowder

You can use fresh, cooked tuna steak for this recipe, if you prefer. The corn kernels, red pepper, and parsley make for a colorful finished dish.

1 Melt the butter in a large, heavy saucepan and add the bell pepper and celery. Cover and cook over a moderate heat, stirring frequently, for 8–10 minutes. When the mixture becomes a little dry, moisten it with the wine.

2 Add the stock, potatoes, and marjoram, partially cover, and simmer for 15 minutes.

3 Stir in the corn kernels and tuna, season to taste with salt and pepper, and simmer gently, uncovered, for an additional 10 minutes. Stir in the parsley, then serve the chowder immediately in warm bowls, with crusty French bread, if desired.

15

PREP

35

COOK

4

SERVES

herby

¼ cup **butter**

1 small **red bell pepper**, cored, seeded, and chopped

1 **celery stick**, thinly sliced

1 tablespoon **dry white wine**

5 cups **Fish Stock** (see page 16)

8 oz **potatoes**, cut into ½ inch cubes

1 teaspoon finely chopped **marjoram**

11½ oz can **corn kernels**, drained

7 oz can **tuna chunks** in brine, drained and shredded

2 tablespoons finely chopped **parsley**

salt and **pepper**

crusty French **bread**, to serve (optional)

2 lb **mussels** and **clams**, scrubbed and debearded

1 lb **small squid**, cleaned, tentacles removed and sliced into rings

1 lb raw medium or large peeled and deveined **shrimp**

3½ lb **whole mixed fish**, cleaned

BROTH:

⅔ cup extra virgin **olive oil**

4 **leeks**, sliced

4 **garlic cloves**, finely chopped

1¼ cups **dry white wine**

pinch of **saffron threads**

1½ lb ripe **plum tomatoes**, roughly chopped

6 **sun-dried tomatoes in oil**, drained and roughly chopped

1 teaspoon **fennel seeds**

1 tablespoon **dried oregano**

2½ cups **water**

30

PREP

45

COOK

6

SERVES

rich

Sicilian fish soup

In coastal areas of Sicily, piles of mixed small fish are especially set aside for fish soup, and there will also be squid, shellfish, and large shrimp. A well-flavored broth is made with saffron and fennel seeds, and the seafood is poached in it. Traditionally, the fish is served first and the broth is ladled on top.

1 Make the broth. Heat the oil in a large, deep, flameproof casserole, add the leeks and garlic and cook over a moderate heat for 5 minutes or until the leeks are softened. Add the wine and boil until reduced by half. Add the saffron, tomatoes, fennel seeds, oregano, and measured water and bring to a boil. Reduce the heat, cover, and simmer for 20 minutes until the tomatoes and oil separate.

2 Put the mussels and clams in a bowl of cold water. Add the squid to the casserole and poach for 3–4 minutes. Remove with a slotted spoon, cover, and keep warm. Add the shrimp and simmer until opaque and cooked. Remove with a slotted spoon and keep warm.

3 Drain the mussels and clams and add to the broth. Cover and cook for a few minutes until they open. Remove with a slotted spoon and keep warm, discarding any that have not opened. Poach the remaining fish until just cooked, then remove from the broth. Arrange the fish on a serving dish with the shellfish and squid on top. Moisten the fish with some of the broth and serve the rest separately.

Seafood soup

Many Spanish dishes can be identified by the presence of nuts, which are used to flavor and thicken sauces. The seafood in this recipe can be varied to suit individual tastes, for example substituting lobsterettes for the lobsters, or cod for the angler fish.

1 Soak the saffron in the boiling stock for 10 minutes. Meanwhile, heat half of the oil in a large, flameproof casserole, add the onion, garlic, thyme, and crushed red peppers and cook over a moderate heat for 10 minutes or until the onion is lightly golden. Pour in the sherry and boil until reduced by half, then add the tomatoes, stock, and a little salt and pepper. Bring to a boil, then reduce the heat, cover, and simmer for 20 minutes. Transfer ⅔ cup of the broth to a bowl and reserve.

2 Discard the lobster heads, cut the bodies in half lengthwise, and separate the claws. Cut the angler fish into cubes and dust lightly with the flour. Scrub and debeard the mussels and scrub the clams. Add all the seafood to the casserole and return to a boil, stirring well. Cover and simmer for an additional 10 minutes or until all the seafood is cooked.

3 Combine the ground almonds, vinegar, remaining oil, and reserved broth and stir into the stew. Cook, stirring, for 5 minutes until thick. Serve in warm soup bowls with crusty bread, accompanied by finger bowls.

30*
PREP

50
COOK

4
SERVES

posh

* Plus 10 minutes soaking

few **saffron threads**

⅔ cup boiling **Fish Stock** (see page 16)

4 tablespoons **olive oil**

1 **onion**, chopped

2 **garlic cloves**, crushed

1 tablespoon chopped **thyme**

¼ teaspoon **crushed red pepper**

½ cup **dry sherry**

13 oz can chopped **tomatoes**

2 small cooked **lobsters**, each about 15 oz

1 lb **angler fish** fillet

2 tablespoons **all-purpose flour**

12 large raw peeled and deveined **shrimp**

1 lb **mussels**

1 lb **clams**

½ cup ground **toasted almonds**

1 tablespoon **sherry vinegar**

salt and **pepper**

crusty **bread**, to serve

fish and shellfish 73

Bouillabaisse

35

PREP

40

COOK

6

SERVES

classic

4 tablespoons **olive oil**

2 **garlic cloves**, finely chopped

2 **onions**, chopped

1 lb prepared **mackerel**, cut into bite-size pieces

1 lb **whiting** fillet, cut into bite-size pieces

1 lb **haddock** or **cod** fillet, cut into bite-size pieces

8 oz raw peeled **shrimp**

6 **tomatoes**, skinned and chopped

½ teaspoon **saffron threads**

6 cups hot **Fish Stock** (see page 16)

1 **bay leaf**

3 sprigs of **parsley**

10–12 **mussels**, scrubbed and debearded

6–8 slices **French bread**

salt and **pepper**

2 tablespoons finely chopped **parsley**, to garnish

This is another classic dish that is somewhere between a soup and a stew because of its chunky consistency and hearty ingredients. The fish will be lovely and tender, and will soak up some of the wonderful juices.

1 Heat the oil in a large, heavy saucepan and add the garlic and onions. Cover and cook over a moderate heat for 5 minutes or until the onions are softened but not browned. Add the mackerel, whiting, haddock or cod, and cook, uncovered and stirring occasionally, for 10 minutes.

2 Add the shrimp and tomatoes. Dissolve the saffron in the boiling stock and add to the pan with the bay leaf, parsley sprigs, and salt and pepper to taste. Stir and bring to a boil. Reduce the heat, cover, and simmer for 15 minutes. Add the mussels and cook for an additional 10 minutes or until the fish is cooked thoroughly.

3 Remove and discard the bay leaf, parsley, and any mussels that have not opened. Place the bread in a warm soup tureen and ladle in the soup. Sprinkle with the chopped parsley before serving.

Philippine sour fish soup

20

PREP

30

COOK

In the Philippines, star fruit, or carambolas, are included in soups and meat dishes for their slightly tart flavor. This soup, known as **sinaging**, is usually served with plain boiled rice.

1 Put the onion, garlic, tomatoes, star fruit, lemon juice, and measured water in a large, heavy saucepan and bring to a fast simmer. Cover and simmer for 20 minutes.

2 Add the fish sauce to the pan and, with the back of a wooden spoon, break up the star fruit pieces into a pulp. Add the fish and simmer gently for 8–10 minutes.

3 Taste the soup and season with salt and pepper if necessary. Serve in large, warm soup bowls with extra fish sauce, lime wedges, and pickled green chilies.

4

SERVES

exotic

1 **onion**, finely chopped

2 **garlic cloves**, crushed

1 lb unripe **tomatoes**, quartered

1 **star fruit**, thickly sliced

4 tablespoons **lemon juice**

5 cups **water**

3 tablespoons **Thai fish sauce**, plus extra to serve

1½ lb **mixed white fish**

salt and **pepper**

TO SERVE:

lime wedges

pickled green chilies

vegetables

1 tablespoon **sunflower oil**

2 lb **pumpkin**, peeled, seeded, and cut into 1 inch cubes

1 **onion**, chopped

1½ cups diced **carrots**

1 **celery stick**, sliced

2 teaspoons **curry powder**

1 tablespoon **whole-wheat flour**

5 cups **Chicken Stock** (see page 17)

8 oz **bacon**, trimmed of fat and diced

salt and **pepper**

TO GARNISH:

pumpkin seeds

grated nutmeg

15

PREP

20

COOK

6

SERVES

tasty

Tuscan pumpkin soup

This quick soup is perfect for a nourishing midweek supper. Pumpkin is becoming more widely popular and rightly so—it's a versatile vegetable that's very nutritious, too.

1 Heat the oil in a large, heavy saucepan, add the pumpkin, onion, carrots, and celery and cook over a moderate heat for 5 minutes or until lightly browned. Stir in the curry powder and cook for an additional 1 minute. Stir in the flour. Remove from the heat and stir in the stock.

2 In a blender or food processor, blend the soup in batches until smooth, then return it to the pan.

3 Heat a dry nonstick skillet, add the bacon and cook over a moderate to high heat, stirring constantly, for 3–4 minutes. Remove with a slotted spoon and drain on paper towels, then add to the soup. Taste and adjust the seasoning if necessary, then bring the soup to a boil. Reduce the heat and simmer, stirring, for 5 minutes.

4 Spoon the soup into warm soup bowls, garnish with pumpkin seeds and nutmeg, and serve immediately.

Pumpkin and coconut soup

15 PREP

25 COOK

4 SERVES

spicy

Coconut milk isn't the liquid you find inside the coconut—that's coconut water. The milk is produced by squeezing the flesh of the coconut, which produces a much thicker and creamier liquid than the water. To make a more substantial dish, serve with naan bread.

1 Heat the oil in a large, heavy saucepan, add the onion, garlic, ginger, chilies, and spices and cook over a moderate heat, stirring frequently, for 10 minutes.

2 Add the pumpkin, stock, coconut milk, tamarind pulp, and cinnamon stick and bring to a boil. Reduce the heat, cover, and simmer gently for 10 minutes, or until the pumpkin is just tender.

3 Remove and discard the cinnamon stick. In a blender or food processor, blend the soup with the fresh cilantro until smooth. Transfer the soup to warm soup bowls and serve immediately, garnished with cilantro leaves and yogurt.

2 tablespoons **sunflower oil**

1 **onion**, chopped

4 **garlic cloves**, crushed

1 inch piece of fresh **gingerroot**, peeled and grated

2 **red chilies**, seeded, and chopped

1 teaspoon **ground coriander**

½ teaspoon **ground cumin**

seeds from 2 **cardamom pods**

1½ lb **pumpkin**, peeled, seeded, and diced

3 cups **Vegetable Stock** (see page 19)

⅔ cup **coconut milk**

1 tablespoon **tamarind pulp**

1 **cinnamon stick**

2 tablespoons chopped fresh **cilantro**, plus extra to garnish

salt and **pepper**

plain yogurt, to garnish

1½ lb **pumpkin**, peeled, seeded, and cut into large cubes

6 **garlic cloves**, unpeeled

4 tablespoons **olive oil**

2 **onions**, thinly sliced

2 **celery sticks**, chopped

¼ cup **white long-grain rice**

6 cups **Vegetable Stock** (see page 19) or **water**

4 tablespoons chopped **parsley**

salt and **pepper**

15

PREP

45

COOK

6

SERVES

thick

Pumpkin and garlic soup

Roasting the pumpkin and garlic together concentrates the flavor of the pumpkin, which can be bland. Look for a variety of pumpkin with bright orange flesh, or try using butternut squash instead.

1 Put the pumpkin in a roasting pan with the garlic and toss with half of the oil. Roast in a preheated oven, 400°F, for 30 minutes or until very tender and beginning to brown.

2 Meanwhile, heat the remaining oil in a large, heavy saucepan, add the onions and celery, and cook over a low heat for 10 minutes or until just beginning to brown. Stir in the rice and stock or water and bring to a boil. Reduce the heat, cover, and simmer for 15–20 minutes or until the rice is tender.

3 Remove the pumpkin and garlic from the oven and allow to cool slightly. Pop the garlic cloves out of their skins and add to the pan with the pumpkin. Bring to a boil, then reduce the heat and simmer for 10 minutes.

4 In a blender or food processor, roughly blend the soup in batches, then return it to the pan. Season to taste with salt and pepper. Add a little more stock or water if the soup is too thick. Reheat gently, then stir in the parsley and serve immediately in warm bowls.

Pumpkin soup with cilantro pistou

Cilantro is used in the pistou (the French word for pesto), replacing the more familiar basil, and adding a North African influence to this Provençal soup.

20

PREP

35

COOK

6

SERVES

herby

1 Arrange the pumpkin, thyme, and garlic in a roasting pan so that they fit snugly in a single layer. Add half of the oil and toss gently to coat. Season to taste with salt and pepper. Roast in a preheated oven, 400°F, for 30 minutes or until charred and tender.

2 Meanwhile, heat the remaining oil in a large, heavy saucepan, add the onion, celery, and chili and cook over a low heat for 10 minutes or until softened. Add the stock and bring to a boil. Reduce the heat, cover, and simmer for 20 minutes. Stir in the roasted pumpkin and return to a boil, then reduce the heat and simmer for 5 minutes.

3 Remove and discard the thyme. In a blender or food processor, blend the soup in batches until really smooth. Keep warm.

4 Put all the ingredients for the pistou in a spice grinder and grind to a smooth paste or use a mortar and pestle. Spoon the soup into warm soup bowls and swirl a little pistou into each one just before serving.

1 lb **pumpkin** flesh, cut into cubes

4 sprigs of **thyme**

4 **garlic cloves**, peeled but left whole

4 tablespoons **olive oil**

1 **onion**, chopped

2 **celery sticks**, sliced

1 **red chili**, seeded and chopped

5 cups **Vegetable Stock** (see page 19)

salt and **pepper**

CILANTRO PISTOU:

¼ cup fresh **cilantro**

1 **garlic clove**, crushed

1 tablespoon **blanched almonds**, chopped

4 tablespoons extra virgin **olive oil**

1 tablespoon grated **Parmesan cheese**

salt and **pepper**

2 tablespoons **olive oil**

1 large **onion**, finely chopped

1 **butternut squash**, about 1¾ lb, peeled, seeded, and cut into cubes

1 **sweet potato**, about 10 oz, peeled and cut into cubes

1½ inch piece of fresh **gingerroot**, peeled and finely chopped

2 **garlic cloves**, chopped (optional)

4 cups **Vegetable Stock** (see page 19)

1¾ cups low fat **milk**

salt and **pepper**

CROUTONS:

1 **poppy seed bagel**, cut into cubes

2 tablespoons **olive oil**

20

PREP

50

COOK

6

SERVES

hearty

Squash, sweet potato, and ginger soup

Velvety smooth, with a wonderful vibrant color, this soup makes an ideal quick lunch and is smart enough to serve to friends, if dressed up with a swirl of cream.

1 Heat the oil in a large, heavy saucepan, add the onion and cook over a moderate heat for about 5 minutes or until softened. Add the butternut squash, sweet potato, ginger, and garlic (if using) and cook, stirring continuously, for 3 minutes.

2 Pour in the stock, season to taste with salt and pepper and bring to a boil. Reduce the heat, cover, and simmer for 30 minutes or until reduced and thickened. In a blender or food processor, blend the soup in batches until smooth, then return it to the pan. Stir in the milk and set aside until ready to reheat.

3 Just before serving, put the bagel cubes into a plastic bag with the oil, toss together and transfer to a baking sheet. Bake in a preheated oven, 400°F, for 10 minutes or until golden. Reheat the soup gently, then ladle into warm bowls and serve immediately sprinkled with the croutons.

Butternut squash and tofu soup

It's unusual in traditional Chinese cooking to find the blended soups so often seen in other parts of the world. This recipe is so creamy that you might think it contains milk or cream. You can use pumpkin instead of the butternut squash if you prefer.

1 Put the onion in a large, heavy saucepan, cover, and allow to sweat over a low heat for 10 minutes.

2 Add the carrots, butternut squash, ginger, and stock and bring to a boil.

3 Reduce the heat and simmer gently for 25–30 minutes until all the vegetables are tender. Add the tofu, stir well, and return the soup to a boil.

4 In a blender or food processor, blend the soup until smooth and creamy. Ladle into warm soup bowls and serve immediately.

15

PREP

45

COOK

4

SERVES

easy

1 large **onion**, roughly chopped

5 oz **carrots**, cut into large cubes

1 **butternut squash**, 1¼–1½ lb, cut into large cubes

1 slice of fresh **gingerroot**

2½ **Vegetable Stock** (see page 19)

1 cup silken **tofu**, roughly chopped

1 lb **chestnuts**

1 tablespoon **olive oil**

4 oz rindless **bacon**, diced

1 large **onion**, chopped

2 **celery sticks**, chopped

2 **carrots**, chopped

1 **bouquet garni**

5 cups **Chicken Stock** (see page 17)

salt and **pepper**

TO GARNISH:

broiled **bacon**, crumbled

chopped **parsley**

40

PREP

75

COOK

8

SERVES

party

Cream of chestnut soup

This simple recipe relies on fresh, quality ingredients. The bacon and chestnuts are given plenty of time to cook, during which they combine to produce a rounded flavor that's unusual but delicious.

1 Cut a slash in the pointed end of each chestnut. Place in a saucepan, cover with cold water, and bring to a boil, then reduce the heat and simmer for 2 minutes. Remove from the heat. Using a slotted spoon, lift out one chestnut at a time and remove and discard the outer and inner skins. If the skins are hard to peel, return the pan to a boil and repeat.

2 Heat the oil in a large, heavy saucepan, add the diced bacon and onion and cook over a moderate heat for 2 minutes without browning. Add the celery, carrots, and bouquet garni and stir well. Add the stock and salt and pepper to taste. Add the peeled chestnuts and bring to a boil. Reduce the heat, cover, and simmer for 1 hour or until the chestnuts are tender. Remove and discard the bouquet garni and allow to cool slightly.

3 In a blender or food processor, blend the soup in batches until smooth, returning to the pan. Reheat gently. Ladle into warm soup bowls, garnish with crumbled broiled bacon and chopped parsley and serve immediately.

Herbed tomato and lemon broth

Plum tomatoes usually have a more intense, tomatoey flavor than other varieties. They work well with spicy ingredients, and the Tabasco sauce gives the soup a lively twist that will be tempered slightly by the fresh oregano and parsley.

5

PREP

30

COOK

4

SERVES

fresh

1 Drain the tomatoes, reserving half of the juice. Melt the butter in a large, heavy saucepan, add the tomatoes and cook over a moderate heat, stirring and breaking them up with a wooden spoon, for 5 minutes.

2 Add the reserved tomato juice, stock, lemon juice and zest, and plenty of pepper. Stir in the sugar, Tabasco or hot pepper sauce, and the Worcestershire sauce. Bring to a boil. Reduce the heat and simmer for 15 minutes.

3 Stir in the oregano and parsley and simmer the soup for an additional 5 minutes.

4 In a blender or food processor, blend the soup until smooth. Reheat briefly in a clean saucepan. Ladle into warm soup bowls, garnish each portion with a lemon slice, and serve immediately.

13 oz can **plum tomatoes**

2 tablespoons) **butter**

2½ cups **Vegetable Stock** (see page 19)

2 tablespoons **lemon juice**

1 teaspoon grated **lemon** zest

½ teaspoon **superfine sugar**

4 drops of **Tabasco sauce** or **hot pepper sauce** (or to taste)

2 teaspoons **Worcestershire sauce**

1 tablespoon chopped **oregano**

1 tablespoon chopped **parsley**

pepper

4 thin **lemon** slices, to garnish

2 lb vine-ripened **tomatoes**, roughly chopped

2 **garlic cloves**, crushed

1¼ **Vegetable Stock** (see page 19)

2 tablespoons extra virgin **olive oil**

1 teaspoon **superfine sugar**

1 cup) **ground almonds**, toasted

salt and **pepper**

BASIL OIL:

⅔ cup extra virgin **olive oil**

1 cup **basil leaves**

15
PREP

20
COOK

4
SERVES

easy

Fresh tomato and almond soup

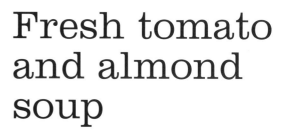

The addition of ground almonds not only flavors this delicious soup but helps to thicken it as well. Make it during the summer months when tomatoes are at their juiciest and best. To toast the almonds, dry-fry them in a skillet over a medium heat, stirring constantly until they are golden brown.

1 Put the tomatoes in a large, heavy saucepan with the garlic, stock, oil, and sugar. Season to taste with salt and pepper. Bring to a boil, then reduce the heat and simmer gently for 15 minutes.

2 Meanwhile, make the basil oil. In a blender or food processor, blend the oil and basil leaves with a pinch of salt until really smooth. Set aside.

3 Stir the ground almonds into the soup, heat through, and then serve in warm soup bowls, drizzled with the basil oil.

Tomato and bread soup

This classic Italian soup is often served at room temperature, but this is a hot version, which brings together the great combination of tomato and basil. If you prefer, you can allow the soup to cool to room temperature before serving.

1 Put the tomatoes in a large, heavy saucepan with the stock, 2 tablespoons of the oil, the garlic, sugar, and basil and slowly bring to a boil. Reduce the heat, cover, and simmer gently for 30 minutes.

2 Crumble the bread into the soup and stir over a low heat until thickened. Stir in the vinegar and the remaining oil and season to taste with salt and pepper. Spoon into warm soup bowls and stir a spoonful of pesto into each bowl before serving, if desired.

15

PREP

40

COOK

4

SERVES

classic

2 lb vine-ripened **tomatoes**, skinned, seeded, and chopped

1¼ cups **Vegetable Stock** (see page 19)

6 tablespoons extra virgin **olive oil**

2 **garlic cloves**, crushed

1 teaspoon **superfine sugar**

2 tablespoons chopped **basil**

4 oz day-old **bread**, without crusts

1 tablespoon **balsamic vinegar**

salt and **pepper**

pesto, to serve (optional)

3 tablespoons **olive oil**

1 **onion**, chopped

1 **carrot**, chopped

2 **celery sticks**, sliced

1 **garlic clove**, chopped

1½ lb peeled and chopped **eggplant**

5 cups **Vegetable Stock** (see page 19)

2 tablespoons roughly chopped **basil**

2 tablespoons grated **Parmesan cheese**

1 tablespoon **medium dry sherry**

½ cup **heavy cream**

salt and **pepper**

25

PREP

75

COOK

4

SERVES

stylish

Eggplant soup

Eggplants are so called because these fruiting vegetables grow to the size and shape of eggs in their native East Indies. They have a distinctive, slightly smoky flavor.

1 Heat the oil in a large, heavy saucepan and add the onion, carrot, celery, garlic, and eggplant. Cover tightly and cook over a low heat, stirring frequently, for 15–18 minutes or until softened.

2 Add the stock and bring to a boil. Reduce the heat, cover, and simmer for 1 hour or until the vegetables are very tender. Add the basil and allow to cool slightly.

3 In a blender or food processor, blend the soup in batches until smooth, then transfer it to a clean saucepan.

4 Stir in the Parmesan, sherry, and cream. Reheat gently without boiling and season to taste with salt and pepper. Ladle into warm soup bowls and serve immediately.

Bright red pepper soup

A vibrant and warming soup, this can be served at any meal and it tastes just as good warm or cold.

15 PREP

40 COOK

4 SERVES

simple

2 tablespoons **olive oil**

2 **onions**, finely chopped

1 **garlic clove**, crushed (optional)

3 **red bell peppers**, cored, seeded, and roughly chopped

2 **zucchini**, roughly chopped

4 cups **Vegetable Stock** (see page 19) or **water**

salt and **pepper**

TO SERVE:

plain yogurt or **heavy cream**

snipped **chives**

1 Heat the oil in a large, heavy saucepan, add the onions and cook over a moderate heat for about 5 minutes or until softened. Add the garlic (if using) and cook, stirring, for 1 minute.

2 Add all the bell peppers and half of the zucchini to the pan and cook for 5–8 minutes or until softened and browned.

3 Add the stock, season to taste with salt and pepper, and bring to a boil. Reduce the heat, cover, and simmer gently for 20 minutes or until the vegetables are tender.

4 In a blender or food processor, blend the soup in batches until smooth, then transfer it to a clean saucepan. Check and adjust the seasoning if necessary. Reheat the soup gently and serve topped with the remaining chopped zucchini, yogurt or a swirl of cream, and snipped chives.

6 large **red bell peppers**

3 tablespoons **olive oil**

4 **leeks**, white and pale green parts only, thinly sliced

3 cups **Vegetable Stock** (see page 19)

⅓ cup **mascarpone cheese**

⅓ cup **milk**

2 teaspoons **black peppercorns**, finely ground

salt and **pepper**

toasted country **bread**, to serve

20[*]

PREP

60

COOK

4

SERVES

spicy

Red pepper soup with pepper cream

The smoky, sweet flavor of roasted peppers is given a pungent kick by the addition of black pepper. Black pepper is fundamental to much Italian cooking, especially in the north.

1 Put the bell peppers in a large roasting pan and roast in a preheated oven, 475°F, for 20–30 minutes, turning once, until beginning to char. Remove from the oven and transfer to a plastic bag. Close tightly and allow to steam for 10 minutes.

2 Remove the peppers from the bag and peel off the skins. Pull out the stalks—the seeds should come with them. Halve, scrape out any remaining seeds, and roughly chop the flesh.

3 Heat the oil in a large, heavy saucepan, add the leeks and cook over a low heat for 10 minutes. Add the peppers, stock, and a little salt and pepper. Bring to a boil. Reduce the heat and simmer for 20 minutes. Meanwhile, in a bowl, beat the mascarpone with the milk and ground peppercorns. Season to taste with salt, cover, and chill.

4 In a blender or food processor, blend the soup in batches until smooth, then transfer it to a clean saucepan. Reheat gently. Serve in warm soup bowls with dollops of the pepper cream and slices of toasted country bread.

* Plus 10 minutes steaming

Roasted pepper and tomato soup

To remove the pepper skins quickly, hold them under cold running water and simply rub the charred skins away. This also makes them cool enough to handle easily.

1 Arrange the bell peppers skin side up and the tomatoes skin side down on a baking sheet and cook under a preheated high broiler for 8–10 minutes until the skins of the peppers are charred. Remove from the broiler and transfer to a plastic bag. Close tightly and allow to steam for 10 minutes. Allow the tomatoes to cool.

2 Remove the peppers from the bag and peel off the skins. Slice the flesh. Peel off the skins of the tomatoes.

3 Heat the oil in a large, heavy saucepan, add the onion and carrot and cook over a moderate heat for 5 minutes. Add the stock, peppers, and tomatoes and bring to a boil, then reduce the heat and simmer for 25 minutes until the carrot is tender.

4 In a blender or food processor, blend the soup in batches until smooth, then put it into a clean saucepan. Reheat gently. Stir through the crème fraîche and basil. Season well with pepper and serve in warm soup bowls.

10*

PREP

45

COOK

4

SERVES

tasty

4 **red bell peppers**, halved, cored, and seeded

1 lb **tomatoes**, halved

1 teaspoon **olive oil**

1 **onion**, chopped

1 **carrot**, chopped

2½ cups **Vegetable Stock** (see page 19)

2 tablespoons reduced fat **crème fraîche**

handful of **basil**, torn into pieces

pepper

* Plus 10 minutes steaming

3 **yellow bell peppers**, halved, cored, and seeded

⅓ cup **butter**

1 small **onion**, chopped

5 cups **Vegetable Stock** (see page 19)

1 teaspoon mild **curry powder**

¼ teaspoon **ground turmeric**

1 tablespoon chopped fresh **cilantro**

2½ cups chopped **potatoes**

salt

PREP **20**

COOK **55**

SERVES **4**

hearty

Yellow pepper soup

Slightly sweet, yellow bell peppers are milder in flavor than green ones. This quick and easy soup is an excellent choice for lunch.

1 Chop half of 1 yellow pepper finely and put in a small saucepan. Chop the remaining peppers roughly.

2 Melt ¼ cup of the butter in a large, heavy saucepan, add the onion and roughly chopped peppers and cook over a moderate heat for 5 minutes. Stir in the stock, curry powder, turmeric, and cilantro, then add the potatoes. Bring to a boil. Reduce the heat, partially cover, and simmer for 40–45 minutes or until the vegetables are tender.

3 Meanwhile, melt the remaining butter with the finely chopped pepper in the small pan. Cook over a low heat until the pepper is very tender. Set aside for the garnish.

4 In a blender or food processor, blend the soup in batches until smooth, then transfer it to a clean saucepan. Reheat gently. Serve in warm soup bowls, garnishing each portion with a little of the finely chopped pepper.

Fennel and lemon soup

20

PREP

40

COOK

4

SERVES

posh

Fennel, lemon, and black olives are a perfect combination of flavors. To give this soup a summery flavor, use fat salad onions, like giant scallions, which you sometimes see in bunches in early summer. Use Greek-style, crinkled black olives with their full ripe fruity flavor for the gremolata.

1 Heat the oil in a large, heavy saucepan, add the scallions and cook over a moderate heat for 5 minutes or until softened. Add the sliced fennel, potato, and lemon zest and cook for 5 minutes or until the fennel begins to soften.

2 Add the stock and bring to a boil. Reduce the heat, cover, and simmer for 25 minutes or until all the vegetables are tender.

3 Meanwhile, make the gremolata. Mix the garlic, lemon zest, fennel fronds, and parsley. Stir in the olives, cover, and chill.

4 In a blender or food processor, blend the soup in batches until smooth. Press through a sieve to remove any remaining strings of fennel and transfer to a clean saucepan. Reheat gently. The soup should not be too thick, so add more stock if necessary. Taste and season well with salt and pepper and plenty of lemon juice. Ladle into warm soup bowls and sprinkle each serving with a portion of the gremolata, which should be stirred in before eating.

⅓ cup extra virgin **olive oil**

3 **large scallions**, chopped

8 oz **fennel**, trimmed and thinly sliced, any fronds reserved and finely chopped for the gremolata

1 **potato**, diced

finely grated zest and juice of 1 **lemon**

3 cups **Vegetable Stock** (see page 19)

salt and **pepper**

BLACK OLIVE GREMOLATA:

1 small **garlic clove**, finely chopped

finely grated zest of 1 **lemon**

4 tablespoons chopped **parsley**

16 Greek-style **black olives**, pitted and chopped

4 cups **Vegetable Stock**
(see page 19)

2 **fennel bulbs**, trimmed
and chopped

1 **onion**, chopped

1 **zucchini**, chopped

1 **carrot**, chopped

2 **garlic cloves**, thinly
sliced

13 oz can **tomatoes**

2 x 13 oz cans **lima
beans**, rinsed and
drained

2 tablespoons chopped
sage

pepper

15

PREP

40

COOK

4

SERVES

easy

Fennel and white bean soup

If you are using fresh tomatoes and have enough time, it's worth removing the skins. To do this, cut a small cross at the top of each tomato and put them in a heatproof bowl of boiling water for a couple of minutes. The skins should peel off easily.

1 Put 1¼ cups of the stock in a large, heavy saucepan and add the fennel, onion, zucchini, carrot, and garlic. Cover and bring to a boil. Boil for 5 minutes. Uncover, reduce the heat, and simmer gently for 20 minutes or until all the vegetables are tender.

2 Stir in the tomatoes, beans, and sage. Season to taste with pepper and pour in the remaining stock. Simmer for 5 minutes, then allow the soup to cool slightly.

3 In a blender or food processor, blend 1¼ cups of the soup until smooth. Return to the pan and reheat gently. Serve the soup immediately in warm soup bowls.

Parsnip and fennel soup

These two flavorsome vegetables make the ideal partnership in this deliciously creamy soup. It makes quite a filling meal, but you should serve it with plenty of warmed bread for dunking.

15

PREP

40

COOK

4

SERVES

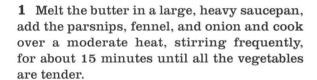

filling

¼ cup **butter**

1 lb **parsnips**, scrubbed and cut into ¼ inch dice

1 lb **fennel bulb**, trimmed and diced

1 **onion**, chopped

3 tablespoons **cornstarch**

5 cups hot **Vegetable Stock** (see page 19)

⅔ cup **heavy cream**

salt and **pepper**

1 Melt the butter in a large, heavy saucepan, add the parsnips, fennel, and onion and cook over a moderate heat, stirring frequently, for about 15 minutes until all the vegetables are tender.

2 In a small bowl, blend the cornstarch with ⅔ cup of the hot stock until thick and smooth. Fold into the vegetables, then pour in the remaining hot stock, stirring the mixture constantly.

3 Bring to a boil, stirring, then reduce the heat, partially cover, and simmer, stirring frequently, for 20 minutes. Season to taste with salt and pepper, stir in the cream and heat through gently without boiling. Serve immediately in warm soup bowls.

2 tablespoons **butter**

2 tablespoons peeled and thinly sliced fresh **gingerroot**

1 bunch of **scallions**

1 lb **parsnips**, sliced

4 cups **Vegetable Stock** (see page 19)

salt and **pepper**

crème fraîche, to serve

10

PREP

20

COOK

4

SERVES

thick

Fresh ginger and parsnip soup

This simple soup has Asian influences. Crème fraîche is a lovely garnish for all manner of soups, as it begins to sink into the hot liquid and adds a cool, creamy taste.

1 Melt the butter in a large, heavy saucepan, add the ginger and cook over a moderate heat, stirring, for 1 minute. Reserve 1 scallion, roughly chop the remainder and add to the pan with the parsnips. Cook, stirring, for 2 minutes.

2 Add the stock and bring to a boil, then reduce the heat, cover, and simmer gently for 15 minutes or until the parsnips are tender. Meanwhile, shred the reserved scallion lengthwise into fine ribbons.

3 In a blender or food processor, blend the soup in batches until smooth, then return it to the pan. Season to taste with salt and pepper and reheat gently for 1 minute.

4 Ladle into warm soup bowls and serve topped with a spoonful of crème fraîche and scattered with the scallion ribbons.

Curried parsnip soup

Parsnips and spices are blended to create a warming soup with an Indian flavor. If you prefer a milder flavor, use less curry powder or choose a milder version.

15

PREP

45

COOK

6

SERVES

spicy

½ cup **butter**

3 lb **parsnips**, scrubbed and roughly chopped

1 **onion**, chopped

1 **potato**, chopped

1 tablespoon medium hot **curry powder**

1 teaspoon **ground turmeric**

½ teaspoon **ground cumin**

7 cups **Vegetable Stock** (see page 19)

⅔ cup **heavy cream**

salt and **pepper**

snipped **chives** or finely chopped **parsley**, to garnish

1 Melt the butter in a large, heavy saucepan, add the parsnips, onion, potato, curry powder, turmeric, and cumin and stir well. Cover and cook over a low to moderate heat, stirring occasionally, for 10 minutes.

2 Add the stock and bring to a boil. Reduce the heat, cover, and simmer for 30 minutes. Add a little water if the soup is too thick.

3 In a blender or food processor, blend the soup in batches, then transfer it to a clean saucepan. Reheat gently and stir in the cream. Serve the soup immediately in warm soup bowls, garnishing each portion with a sprinkling of chives or parsley.

2 tablespoons **olive oil**

1 **onion**, finely chopped

1 **baking potato**, about
9 oz, diced

1 **garlic clove**, chopped

7 oz can **tomatoes**

4 cups **Vegetable Stock**
(see page 19)

6 oz **broccoli**, cut into
tiny florets and stalks
sliced

1¼ cups frozen **peas**

2 teaspoons **pesto**, plus
extra to garnish

salt and **pepper**

TO GARNISH:

grated **Parmesan cheese**

handful of **basil** leaves

15

PREP

30

COOK

4

SERVES

herby

Quick pesto, pea, and broccoli soup

This hearty vegetable soup is full of Italian flavor. If you prefer, use four fresh, skinned and chopped tomatoes instead of the canned tomatoes. To make the soup more substantial, add a small can of cannellini or white kidney beans, or small soup pasta.

1 Heat the oil in a large, heavy saucepan, add the onion and cook over a moderate heat for 5–6 minutes or until lightly browned. Add the potato and garlic and cook, stirring frequently, for about 5 minutes or until the potato is softened.

2 Add the tomatoes and stock, season to taste with salt and pepper and bring to a boil. Reduce the heat, cover, and simmer for 10 minutes or until reduced and thickened. Add the broccoli, peas, and pesto and simmer for an additional 3–4 minutes or until the broccoli is just tender.

3 Ladle the soup into warm soup bowls. Serve garnished with a little extra pesto, grated Parmesan, and basil leaves.

Creamy broccoli and almond soup

Keep a watchful eye on the clock while you're making this soup because overcooking will result in a duller green soup, not the pretty, speckled green effect you're aiming at. If you prefer, use lowfat milk and lowfat cream cheese for a lighter result.

20

PREP

20

COOK

4

SERVES

rich

1 tablespoon **butter**

1 tablespoon **olive oil**

1 **onion**, roughly chopped

1¼ cups finely diced **potato**

10 oz **broccoli**

1¾ cups **Vegetable Stock** (see page 19)

3 tablespoons **slivered almonds**

1¾ cups **milk**

½ cup **cream cheese**

grated **nutmeg**, to taste

salt and **pepper**

TO GARNISH:

2 tablespoons **slivered almonds**, toasted

a little **paprika**

1 Heat the butter and oil in a large, heavy saucepan, add the onion and potato and cook over a moderate heat for 5 minutes or until softened but not browned.

2 Cut the broccoli into florets and slice the stalks. Add to the pan together with the stock and bring to a boil. Reduce the heat, cover, and simmer for 8 minutes or until all the vegetables are just tender.

3 In a blender or food processor, blend the soup with the almonds, milk, and cream cheese in batches until smooth, then return it to the pan. Season to taste with salt and pepper and nutmeg. Reheat gently without boiling. Ladle the soup into warm soup bowls. Serve garnished with the toasted slivered almonds and paprika.

2 lb **green broccoli**

¼ cup **butter**

1 **onion**, chopped

1 large **potato**, quartered

1 tablespoon medium hot **curry powder**

6 cups **Vegetable Stock** (see page 19)

⅔ cup **light cream**

salt and **pepper**

15

PREP

35

COOK

6

SERVES

thick

Curried cream of broccoli soup

There are several types of broccoli available, including purple- and white-flowered forms. In this soup, green broccoli, or calabrese, is used. Try not to overcook it, which will spoil the flavor.

1 Cut off the broccoli stalks, peel and slice them into 1 inch pieces. Break the florets into very small pieces and reserve.

2 Melt the butter in a large, heavy saucepan and add the onion and broccoli stalks. Cover and cook over a moderate heat, stirring frequently, for 5 minutes.

3 Add the reserved florets, potato, curry powder, and stock. Bring to a boil, partially cover, and cook for 5 minutes. Using a slotted spoon, remove 6 florets for the garnish and reserve. Season with salt and pepper. Cook over a moderate heat for an additional 20 minutes or until all the vegetables are tender.

4 In a blender or food processor, blend the soup in batches until smooth, then transfer it to a clean saucepan. Add the cream and reheat gently without boiling. Serve the soup in warm bowls, garnishing each one with some of the reserved florets.

Broccoli and cheese soup

PREP 15

This is a variation of Curried Cream of Broccoli Soup (opposite). The cream and cheese make this quite a rich, thick soup, so if you're serving it as an appetizer, you will need only a small amount per person.

COOK 35

1 Cut off the broccoli stalks, peel and slice them into 1 inch pieces. Break the florets into very small pieces and reserve.

2 Melt the butter in a large, heavy saucepan and add the onion and broccoli stalks. Cover and cook over a moderate heat, stirring frequently, for 5 minutes.

3 Add the reserved florets, potato, curry powder, and stock. Bring to a boil, partially cover, and cook for 5 minutes. Using a slotted spoon, remove 6 florets for the garnish and reserve. Season to taste with salt and pepper. Cook over a moderate heat for 20 minutes or until all the vegetables are tender.

4 In a blender or food processor, blend the soup in batches until smooth, then transfer it to a clean saucepan. Add the cream, lemon juice, Worcestershire sauce, and Tabasco sauce. Simmer gently for 3–5 minutes without boiling. Stir in the grated cheese, then serve immediately in warm soup bowls.

SERVES 6

thick

2 lb **green broccoli**

¼ cup **butter**

1 **onion**, chopped

1 large **potato**, quartered

6 cups **Vegetable Stock** (see page 19)

½ cup **light cream**

1 tablespoon **lemon juice**

1 teaspoon **Worcestershire sauce**

few drops of **Tabasco sauce** (or to taste)

4 oz mature **cheddar cheese**, grated

salt and **pepper**

¼ cup **butter**

2 tablespoons **olive oil**

1 **onion**, diced

1 **garlic clove**, chopped

2 **potatoes**, chopped

8 oz **broccoli**, chopped

10 oz **spinach**, chopped

4 cups **Vegetable Stock** (see page 19)

4 oz **Gorgonzola cheese**, crumbled into small pieces

2 tablespoons **lemon juice**

½ teaspoon **grated nutmeg**

salt and **pepper**

¾ cup toasted **pine nuts**, to garnish

warm crusty **bread**, to serve

10

PREP

20

COOK

4

SERVES

simple

Spinach and broccoli soup

Spinach and blue cheese are a match made in heaven! The cheese will start to melt into the liquid and can be mopped up with warm crusty bread.

1 Melt the butter with the oil in a large, heavy saucepan, then add the onion and garlic and cook over a moderate heat for about 3 minutes.

2 Add the potatoes, broccoli, spinach, and stock and bring to a boil. Reduce the heat and simmer for 15 minutes.

3 The soup can be blended at this stage in a blender or food processor or left with chunky pieces. Add the Gorgonzola with the lemon juice, nutmeg, and salt and pepper to taste. Garnish with the toasted pine nuts and serve immediately with warm crusty bread.

Spinach and mushroom soup

This is a great way to enjoy mushrooms. The soup is left unblended so that they retain their texture. Make sure you use baby spinach, because the leaves are smaller and more delicate, making them better suited to this particular recipe.

1 Melt the butter with the oil in a large, heavy saucepan, add the onion and cook over a moderate heat for 5 minutes. Add the mushrooms and garlic and cook, stirring, for 3 minutes.

2 Stir in the ginger and stock. Bring to a boil, then reduce the heat, cover, and simmer gently for 10 minutes.

3 Add the spinach and nutmeg and simmer gently for 2 minutes. Season to taste with salt and pepper and serve immediately in warm soup bowls, scattered with croutons.

5

PREP

20

COOK

4

SERVES

light

¼ cup **butter**

1 tablespoon **peanut oil** or **vegetable oil**

1 **onion**, finely chopped

5 oz **shiitake mushrooms**

6 oz **chestnut mushrooms** or **cup mushrooms**

2 **garlic cloves**, crushed

2 inch piece of fresh **gingerroot**, peeled and grated

4 cups **Vegetable Stock** (see page 19)

5 cups **baby spinach**

plenty of **grated nutmeg**

salt and **pepper**

croutons, to serve

2 tablespoons extra virgin **olive oil**, plus extra to serve

1 **onion**, finely chopped

2 **garlic cloves**, finely chopped

10 oz **baby spinach**, roughly shredded

1½ pints **Vegetable Stock**
(see page 19)

6 oz **arborio rice**

4 **eggs**

salt and **pepper**

grated **Parmesan cheese**, to serve (optional)

PREP

COOK

SERVES

Spinach and rice soup

This delicious, hearty soup contains poached eggs, making it a nutritious meal in itself. Poaching the eggs in the soup is also a great way to save time—and it saves on the washing up, too!

1 Heat the oil in a large, heavy saucepan, add the onion and garlic and cook over a moderate heat for 5 minutes or until softened. Add the spinach and cook, stirring well, until wilted.

2 Add the stock and rice and season to taste with salt and pepper. Bring to a boil, then reduce the heat, cover, and simmer gently for 15 minutes or until the rice is tender.

3 Carefully break the eggs into the soup so that they sit on the surface. Cover and cook gently for 5–6 minutes or until the eggs are poached. Serve the soup in warm soup bowls, drizzled with a little extra olive oil and some grated Parmesan, if desired.

Spinach and potato soup

Although frozen leaf spinach can be used for this recipe, the full-flavored taste of fresh spinach cannot be equaled.

1 Melt the butter in a large, heavy saucepan, add the onion and cook over a moderate heat for 5 minutes or until softened but not browned. Add the spinach and cook, stirring, until wilted.

2 Add the stock, potatoes, lemon juice, and nutmeg and season to taste with salt and pepper. Bring to a boil, then reduce the heat, partially cover, and simmer for 10–12 minutes or until the potatoes are tender.

3 In a blender or food processor, blend the soup in batches until smooth, then transfer it to a clean saucepan. Add the cream and reheat gently without boiling. Serve the soup in warm bowls, garnished with a sprinkling of ground almonds, if liked.

10

PREP

20

COOK

4

SERVES

rich

¼ cup **butter**

1 **onion**, finely chopped

1 lb fresh or frozen **spinach**

5 cups **Vegetable Stock** (see page 19)

8 oz **potatoes**, thinly sliced

1 teaspoon **lemon juice**

pinch of **grated nutmeg**

⅔ cup **heavy cream**

salt and **white pepper**

ground almonds, to garnish (optional)

1 tablespoon **olive oil**

1 small **red onion**, finely chopped

1 **garlic clove**, finely chopped

1 **carrot**, diced

2 **celery sticks**, chopped

13 oz can chopped **tomatoes**

1 tablespoon **sun-dried tomato paste**

2½ cups **Vegetable Stock** (see page 19)

1½ lb can **mixed beans**, drained and rinsed

3 tablespoons chopped **flat leaf parsley**

salt and **pepper**

pesto, to serve

10

PREP

40

COOK

4

SERVES

filling

Tuscan bean soup

This rustic soup is based on the classic Italian version and uses the common combination of tomatoes, onion, and garlic as a base. Mixed beans provide the bulk for the soup, and you can either use a can of mixed beans or the equivalent weight of your own choosing.

1 Heat the oil in a large, heavy saucepan, add the onion and cook over a moderate heat for about 5 minutes or until softened. Stir in the garlic, carrot, and celery and cook for 5 minutes.

2 Add the tomatoes, tomato paste, and stock. Season to taste with salt and pepper. Bring to a boil, then reduce the heat and simmer, stirring occasionally, for 20–30 minutes or until the vegetables are tender.

3 In a blender or food processor, blend half of the soup until smooth. Return to the pan. Add the beans to the soup and simmer for an additional 10 minutes until heated through. Stir in the parsley, then serve immediately in warm soup bowls, garnished with a spoonful of pesto.

Chili bean soup

This is a soup version of vegetarian chili, and it is packed full of lovely warming spices. The tortilla chip and melted cheese topping makes an unusual garnish and should help turn this into a family favorite.

1 Heat the oil in a large, heavy saucepan, add the onion, garlic, chili powder, coriander, and cumin and cook over a moderate heat, stirring frequently, for about 5 minutes until the onion has softened. Add the beans, tomatoes, and stock and season with salt and pepper.

2 Bring to a boil, then reduce the heat, cover, and simmer for 15 minutes.

3 In a blender or food processor, blend the soup in batches until fairly smooth. Pour into ovenproof soup bowls.

4 Arrange the tortilla chips on top of the soup, sprinkle with the grated cheese, and cook under a preheated high broiler for 1–2 minutes or until the cheese has melted. Serve the soup immediately with sour cream.

10

PREP

25

COOK

3

SERVES

feast

2 tablespoons **olive oil**

1 **onion**, chopped

1 **garlic clove**, crushed

1 teaspoon hot **chili powder**

1 teaspoon **ground coriander**

½ teaspoon **ground cumin**

13 oz can **red kidney beans**, rinsed and drained

13 oz can chopped **tomatoes**

2½ cups **Vegetable Stock** (see page 19)

12 **tortilla chips**

2 oz **cheddar cheese**, grated

salt and **pepper**

sour cream, to serve

3 tablespoons **olive oil**

1 **onion**, finely chopped

2 **celery sticks**, thinly sliced

2 **garlic cloves**, thinly sliced

2 x 14 oz cans **lima beans**, rinsed and drained

4 tablespoons **sun-dried tomato paste**

4 cups **Vegetable Stock** (see page 19)

1 tablespoon chopped **rosemary** or **thyme**

salt and **pepper**

Parmesan cheese shavings, to serve

5

PREP

20

COOK

4

SERVES

easy

Lima bean and sun-dried tomato soup

Although it takes only a few minutes to make, this chunky soup distinctly resembles a robust Italian minestrone. It will make a worthy main course served with bread and plenty of Parmesan.

1 Heat the oil in a large, heavy saucepan, add the onion and cook over a moderate heat for about 5 minutes until softened. Add the celery and garlic and cook, stirring well, for 2 minutes.

2 Add the beans, tomato paste, stock, and rosemary or thyme. Season to taste with salt and pepper and bring to a boil. Reduce the heat, cover, and simmer gently for 15 minutes. Serve in warm soup bowls sprinkled with Parmesan shavings.

Smooth red bean soup

The red kidney beans, chili and tomatoes give this recipe a real Mexican flavor. If you don't have much time but would still like to make the soup, you could use canned beans instead of dried.

15*

PREP

100

COOK

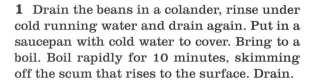

6

SERVES

thick

1 Drain the beans in a colander, rinse under cold running water and drain again. Put in a saucepan with cold water to cover. Bring to a boil. Boil rapidly for 10 minutes, skimming off the scum that rises to the surface. Drain.

2 Heat the oil in a large, heavy saucepan, add the onion, garlic, bell pepper, and carrot and cook over a moderate heat for 5 minutes. Add all the spices and herbs, stock, measured water, beans, tomato paste, and tomatoes and stir well to break up the tomatoes. Bring to a boil, then reduce the heat, partially cover, and simmer for 1¼ hours, skimming off any scum that rises to the surface. Remove and discard the bay leaf.

3 In a blender or food processor, blend the soup until smooth, then strain through a sieve into a clean saucepan. Add salt to taste. Add a little more water if the soup is too thick. Reheat gently without boiling. Serve in warm soup bowls, garnishing each portion with a swirl of sour cream.

¾ cup dried red **kidney beans**, soaked overnight in cold water

3 tablespoons **olive oil**

1 **onion**, chopped

2 **garlic cloves**, chopped

1 **red bell pepper**, cored, seeded, and chopped

1 **carrot**, chopped

¼ teaspoon **cayenne pepper**

1 teaspoon mild **chili powder**

¼ teaspoon **dried thyme**

1 **bay leaf**

1 small sprig of **rosemary**

2½ cups **Vegetable Stock** (see page 19)

5 cups **water**

2 tablespoons **tomato paste**

13 oz can peeled **plum tomatoes**

salt

⅔ cup **sour cream**, to garnish

* Plus overnight soaking

3 tablespoons **olive oil**

2 **onions**, sliced

2 **bay leaves**

¾ cup **green lentils**, washed and drained

4 cups **Vegetable Stock** (see page 19)

½ teaspoon **ground turmeric**

small handful of fresh **cilantro**, roughly chopped

salt and **pepper**

SPICED BUTTER:

¼ cup lightly salted **butter**, softened

1 large **garlic clove**, crushed

1 teaspoon **paprika**

1 teaspoon **cumin seeds**

1 **red chili**, seeded and thinly sliced

PREP

COOK

4

SERVES

spicy

Green lentil soup with spiced butter

Serve the spicy butter separately for stirring into the soup, so that each person can "gee up" their own portion according to personal taste.

1 Heat the oil in a large, heavy saucepan, add the onions and cook over a moderate heat for 3 minutes. Add the bay leaves, lentils, stock, and turmeric. Bring to a boil, then reduce the heat, cover, and simmer for 20 minutes or until the lentils are tender and turning mushy.

2 Meanwhile, make the spiced butter. In a bowl, beat the butter with the remaining ingredients. Transfer to a small serving dish.

3 Stir the cilantro into the soup, season to taste with salt and pepper and serve with the spiced butter in a separate bowl at the table for stirring into the soup.

Lentil and pea soup with crème fraîche

Be sure to use homemade vegetable stock in this recipe. The extra effort is more than made up for by the extra depth of flavor, and if you make a particularly large batch, you can always freeze it.

1 Heat the oil in a large, heavy saucepan, add the leek and garlic and cook over a moderate heat for 5–6 minutes until the leek is softened.

2 Add the lentils, stock, and herbs and bring to a boil. Reduce the heat and simmer for 10 minutes. Add the peas and cook for an additional 5 minutes.

3 In a blender or food processor, blend half of the soup until smooth. Return to the pan. Reheat gently and season well with pepper.

4 Stir the crème fraîche and mint together. Ladle the soup into warm soup bowls and serve, each portion garnished with a dollop of the minty crème fraîche.

10
PREP

25
COOK

4
SERVES

herby

1 teaspoon **olive oil**

1 **leek**, thinly sliced

1 **garlic clove**, crushed

13 oz can **Puy lentils**, drained

5 cups **Vegetable Stock** (see page 19)

2 tablespoons chopped **mixed herbs**, such as thyme and parsley

2 cups frozen **peas**

pepper

TO GARNISH:

2 tablespoons reduced fat **crème fraîche**

1 tablespoon chopped **mint**

3 tablespoons **olive oil**

4 large **onions**, finely chopped

5 cups **Vegetable Stock** (see page 19)

2 teaspoons chopped **thyme**

1 tablespoon chopped **parsley**

salt and **pepper**

GARLIC CROUTONS:

8–12 thick slices of French or Italian **bread**

1 small **garlic clove**, halved

2 tablespoons **olive oil**

2 tablespoons grated **Parmesan cheese** or **cheddar cheese**

20

PREP

60

COOK

4

SERVES

classic

Onion soup with garlic croutons

A slowly cooked onion soup is warming and uplifting in the middle of winter. The onions cook to a sweet, caramelized flavor, and the allium connection is maintained by serving the soup with garlic croutons.

1 Heat the oil in a large, heavy saucepan, add the onions and cook over a low to moderate heat, stirring occasionally, for 20 minutes or until soft and golden brown.

2 Add the stock and thyme and bring to a boil. Boil for 2 minutes, then reduce the heat, cover, and simmer for 30 minutes. Season to taste with salt and pepper.

3 In a blender or food processor, blend the soup in batches until smooth. Return to the pan. Reheat gently and add the parsley.

4 Meanwhile, make the croutons. Lay the slices of bread on a baking sheet and toast under a preheated moderate broiler until golden brown. Rub the top of each slice with the cut side of the garlic clove. Drizzle with the oil and sprinkle with the grated cheese.

5 Cook the bread under the broiler until the cheese just begins to melt. Serve the soup in warm bowls, with the croutons separately, or float them on top of each bowl.

White onion soup

This soup makes the most of the intense flavor and bite of Spanish onions. They are cooked slowly, with milk and cream adding a contrasting texture.

5

PREP

35

COOK

6

SERVES

easy

¼ cup **butter**

6 Spanish **onions**, thickly sliced

1 tablespoon **all-purpose flour**

1¼ cups boiling **water**

4 cups warm **milk**

1 tablespoon **light cream**

salt and **white pepper**

1 Melt the butter in a large, heavy saucepan, add the onions and cook over a high heat, stirring constantly, for 3 minutes without browning. Stir in the flour and cook, stirring constantly, for 1 minute. Gradually stir in the measured boiling water.

2 Season to taste with salt and pepper. Cook over a moderate heat, stirring occasionally, for 10 minutes.

3 Gradually add the milk to the pan, stirring constantly, then cover and simmer gently for 15–20 minutes or until the onions are very tender. Taste and adjust the seasoning if necessary. Stir in the cream and serve in warm soup bowls.

2 tablespoons **butter**

8 oz **scallions**, finely chopped

3 tablespoons **all-purpose flour**

5 cups **Vegetable Stock** (see page 19)

1 tablespoon chopped **basil**

pinch of **grated nutmeg**

⅔ cup **light cream**

salt and **pepper**

1 tablespoon finely chopped **scallion tops**, to garnish

10 PREP

20 COOK

4 SERVES

quick

Scallion soup

This is an amazingly quick and easy recipe to prepare. If you like onion soup, it makes a great alternative for a change. The soup isn't blended, so it offers an interesting bite from the scallions.

1 Heat the butter in a large, heavy saucepan, add the scallions and cook over a moderate heat for about 5 minutes or until softened.

2 Sprinkle in the flour and cook, stirring constantly, for 1 minute. Gradually add the stock, beating vigorously. Add the basil and nutmeg. Season to taste with salt and pepper. Simmer, stirring frequently, for 10 minutes or until slightly thickened.

3 Stir in the cream and heat through gently without boiling. Serve the soup immediately in warm bowls, garnishing each portion with a sprinkling of scallion tops.

Truffled leek and potato soup

A drizzle of luxurious truffle oil transforms this simple soup into something very special. Truffles are prized among all fungi for their intense flavor and aroma—and although the oil is expensive, you need only a little drizzle and the taste is sublime.

1 Heat the butter in a saucepan, add the onion, garlic, and leeks and cook over a moderate heat for 5 minutes. Stir in the potatoes and stock. Season to taste with salt and pepper. Bring to a boil, then reduce the heat, cover, and simmer for 20 minutes.

2 In a blender or food processor, blend the soup in batches until really smooth, then return it to the pan. Reheat gently and taste and adjust the seasoning if necessary. Serve the soup in warm soup bowls, drizzled with truffle oil and sprinkled with snipped chives.

10

PREP

30

COOK

4

SERVES

posh

¼ cup **butter**

1 **onion**, chopped

1 **garlic clove**, crushed

3 **leeks**, about 12 oz trimmed weight, sliced

2½ cups diced **potatoes**

4 cups **Vegetable Stock** (see page 19)

salt and **pepper**

TO GARNISH:

truffle oil

snipped **chives**

Pasta in broth

2 tablespoons **olive oil**

1 small **onion**, finely chopped

1 **celery stick**, finely chopped

several sprigs of **thyme**

1 small glass of **white wine**

6 cups **Vegetable**, **Chicken,** or **Beef Stock** (see pages 17–19)

8 oz fresh **ravioli**, **tortellini,** or **cappelletti**

2–3 tablespoons finely chopped **parsley** or **basil**

salt and **pepper**

grated or shaved **Parmesan cheese**, to serve

PREP 10

20 COOK

4 SERVES

simple

Pasta cooked in broth can be as simple or as elaborate as you like. Use your own specially made stuffed meat or cheese pasta, or cheat and buy ready made for a speedy supper dish.

1 Heat the oil in a large saucepan and fry the onion, celery, and thyme over a gentle heat for 5 minutes.

2 Add the wine and stock and bring slowly to a boil. Reduce the heat and cook gently, uncovered, for 5 minutes.

3 Return the broth to the boil and drop in the pasta. Cook for 5 minutes. Test by lifting out one piece and cutting it in half. The pasta should be just tender and the filling cooked through.

4 Stir in the parsley or basil and season to taste with salt and pepper. Ladle the broth into warm bowls and serve sprinkled with plenty of Parmesan.

Garlic soup with a floating egg

This soup is based on a Spanish dish in which the eggs are poached or oven-baked in a rich, garlicky broth. Here, pasta is added to give a little more substance to the dish.

1 Heat the oil in a large, heavy saucepan, add the bread slices and cook over a moderate heat, turning once, until golden brown. Remove with a slotted spoon and drain on paper towels.

2 Add the garlic, onion, paprika, and cumin to the pan and cook, stirring, for 3 minutes. Add the saffron and stock and bring to a boil. Stir in the pasta, then reduce the heat, cover, and simmer for 8 minutes or until the pasta is just tender. Season with salt and pepper.

3 Break the eggs onto a saucer and slide them into the pan, one at a time. Cook for 2–3 minutes until poached.

4 Stack 3 slices of fried bread in each of 4 soup bowls. Ladle the soup over the bread, making sure each serving contains an egg. Serve immediately.

5

PREP

15

COOK

4

SERVES

stylish

4 tablespoons **olive oil**

12 thick slices of **baguette**

5 **garlic cloves**, sliced

1 **onion**, finely chopped

1 tablespoon **paprika**

1 teaspoon **ground cumin**

good pinch of **saffron threads**

5 cups **Vegetable Stock** (see page 19)

1 oz dried soup **pasta**

4 **eggs**

salt and **pepper**

4 tablespoons **olive oil**

12 oz **shallots**, sliced

1 **red onion**, roughly chopped

2 **garlic cloves**, roughly chopped

4 large sprigs of **rosemary**

1 teaspoon **superfine sugar**

3 cups **Vegetable Stock** (see page 19)

5 tablespoons **heavy cream**

salt and **pepper**

toasted French bread **croutons**, to serve

10

PREP

20

COOK

4

SERVES

herby

Shallot and rosemary soup

This smooth soup makes a good stand-by for vegetarian suppers. If you don't want to make croutons, serve this with plenty of crusty French bread.

1 Heat the oil in a saucepan, add the shallots, onion, garlic, rosemary, and sugar and cook over a moderate heat for 5 minutes or until softened and lightly browned.

2 Add the stock and bring to a boil. Reduce the heat, cover, and simmer gently for about 15 minutes until the shallots are tender.

3 In a blender or food processor, blend the soup in batches until smooth, then return it to the pan.

4 Stir in the cream and season to taste with salt and pepper. Reheat gently for 1 minute, then ladle the soup into warm soup bowls and serve sprinkled with croutons.

Zucchini soup

PREP 10

This soup, which couldn't be easier to make, is delicious served cold in summer, as the lemon gives it a really fresh clean taste.

COOK 30

1 Heat the oil in a large, heavy saucepan, add the shallots and garlic and cook over a moderate heat for 3 minutes.

2 Add the zucchini, potatoes, and stock and bring to a boil. Reduce the heat and simmer for 15 minutes.

3 In a blender or food processor, blend the soup in batches until smooth, or press it through a sieve, then return it to the pan.

4 Add the pasta and simmer for 7 minutes or until just tender. Stir in the lemon zest and juice and chives, then season to taste with salt and pepper. Serve the soup immediately in warm soup bowls.

SERVES 4

fresh

2 tablespoons **olive oil**

4 **shallots**, diced

1 **garlic clove**, crushed

6 **zucchini**, diced

2 **potatoes**, chopped

5 cups **Chicken Stock** (see page 17)

3 oz **farfallini** or other small pasta shapes

juice and zest of 1 **lemon**

large handful of **chives**, snipped

salt and **pepper**

2 tablepoons **butter**

1 tablespoon **olive oil**

1 large **onion**, chopped

1 lb **zucchini**, sliced

¾ cup **pine nuts**

1 tablespoon chopped **sage**

4 cups **Vegetable Stock** (see page 19)

4 oz **Parmesan cheese**, crumbled

4 tablespoons **heavy cream**

salt and **pepper**

10

PREP

15

COOK

4

SERVES

quick

Zucchini and Parmesan soup

It's worth buying a good-quality Parmesan for this recipe, as it's a key ingredient. The Italian theme continues with the pine nuts, which are usually toasted or fried to bring out their flavor.

1 Melt the butter with the oil in a large, heavy saucepan, add the onion, zucchini, and pine nuts and cook over a moderate heat for 5 minutes or until softened.

2 Add the sage and stock and bring to a boil, then reduce the heat, cover, and simmer gently for 5 minutes. Add the Parmesan and cook for an additional 2 minutes.

3 In a blender or food processor, blend the soup in batches until partially blended but not smooth, then return it to the pan.

4 Stir in the cream and season to taste with salt and pepper. Reheat gently for 1 minute, then serve in warm soup bowls.

Zucchini soup with fresh ginger

Fresh gingerroot, so popular in Asian cooking, livens up the flavor of this soup, which would otherwise be dominated by the slight blandness of the zucchini.

1 Trim the zucchini and slice thickly into a colander. Sprinkle with salt and allow to drain for 10–15 minutes. Rinse under cold running water, drain thoroughly and pat dry with paper towels.

2 Melt the butter in a large, heavy saucepan, add the onions and cook over a moderate heat for 5 minutes or until softened. Add the zucchini and cook over a low heat, stirring frequently, for 5 minutes.

3 Add the stock, ginger, and nutmeg and season to taste with pepper. Bring to a boil and add the potatoes, then reduce the heat, partially cover, and simmer for about 40–45 minutes until the vegetables are tender.

4 In a blender or food processor, blend the soup in batches until smooth, then transfer it to a clean saucepan. Reheat gently, then serve in warm soup bowls with a swirl of cream on each portion.

20* PREP

55 COOK

6 SERVES

tasty

3 lb small **zucchini**

¼ cup **butter**

1 cup chopped **onions**

4 cups **Vegetable Stock** (see page 19)

1 tablespoon grated fresh **gingerroot**

pinch of **grated nutmeg**

3 cups chopped **potatoes**

salt and **pepper**

⅔ cup **light cream**, to serve

* Plus 10–15 minutes draining

2 tablespoons **butter**

1 large **onion**, finely chopped

4 cups frozen **peas**

2 **Little Gem or small butterhead lettuces**, roughly chopped

4 cups **Vegetable Stock** (see page 19)

grated zest and juice of ½ **lemon**

salt and **pepper**

SESAME CROUTONS:

2 thick slices of **bread**, cut into cubes

1 tablespoon **olive oil**

1 tablespoon **sesame seeds**

10

PREP

25

COOK

4

SERVES

light

Pea, lettuce, and lemon soup

Lettuce might seem an unusual ingredient for a soup, but it's actually very good cooked. This is a light, refreshing soup that would be ideal for a summer lunch.

1 Make the croutons. Brush the bread cubes with the oil and spread out in a roasting pan. Sprinkle with the sesame seeds and bake in a preheated oven, 400°F, for 10–15 minutes or until golden.

2 Meanwhile, melt the butter in a large, heavy saucepan, add the onion and cook over a moderate heat for 5 minutes or until softened. Add the peas, lettuce, stock, lemon zest and juice, and salt and pepper to taste. Bring to a boil, then reduce the heat, cover, and simmer for 10–15 minutes.

3 In a blender or food processor, blend the soup in batches until smooth, then return it to the pan. Taste and adjust the seasoning if necessary. Reheat gently. Ladle into warm soup bowls and serve sprinkled with the sesame croutons.

Pea and mint soup

Mint is one of the easiest herbs to grow, whether you have space for plants in your garden borders or room on a balcony or by the back door for a single container. Use the fresh leaves all year round in salads or as a garnish, or, as here, in a summery soup.

1 Melt the butter in a large, heavy saucepan, add the onion and cook over a moderate heat for 5 minutes or until softened.

2 Add the peas, sugar, stock, and 3 tablespoons of the chopped mint. Add pepper to taste and bring to a boil. Add the potatoes, then reduce the heat, partially cover, and simmer for 20–25 minutes.

3 In a blender or food processor, blend the soup in batches, then transfer it to a clean saucepan. Season to taste with salt, add the cream and stir well. Reheat gently without boiling. Serve in warm soup bowls, garnished with the remaining mint.

10

PREP

35

COOK

6

SERVES

classic

¼ cup **butter**

1 small **onion**, chopped

1 lb frozen **peas**

¼ teaspoon **superfine sugar**

5 cups **Vegetable Stock** (see page 19)

4 tablespoons chopped **mint**

2½ cups roughly chopped **potatoes**

⅔ cup **heavy cream**

salt and **white pepper**

¼ cup **butter**

1 lb **cucumbers**, peeled, seeded, and cut into ½ inch pieces

2½ cups **peas**, fresh or frozen

pinch of **superfine sugar**

¼ teaspoon **white pepper**

3 tablespoons finely chopped **mint**

5 cups **Vegetable Stock** (see page 19)

1½ cups chopped **potatoes**

⅔ cup **heavy cream**

salt

15*

PREP

30

COOK

6

SERVES

fresh

* Plus 3 hours chilling if served cold

Mint, cucumber, and green pea soup

There's a strong green theme in this tasty summer soup. Opt for fresh peas in the pod, as part of the fun is shelling them. Mint is the perfect partner for peas, and the cucumbers give a light, fresh flavor.

1 Heat the butter in a large, heavy saucepan, add the cucumber and cook over a moderate heat for 5 minutes. Add the peas, sugar, pepper, and 2 tablespoons of the mint. Pour in the stock and bring to a boil, then add the potatoes. Reduce the heat, partially cover, and simmer for 20 minutes or until the potatoes are tender.

2 In a blender or food processor, blend the soup in batches until smooth, then transfer it to a clean saucepan or, if it is to be served cold, to a bowl. Season to taste with salt.

3 If the soup is to be served hot, add the cream and reheat gently without boiling. Serve in warm soup bowls, garnishing each portion with a little of the remaining mint.

4 If the soup is to be served cold, cover the bowl closely and chill for at least 3 hours, making sure that the cream is also chilled. Just before serving, fold in the chilled cream. Serve in chilled bowls, garnishing each portion with some of the remaining mint.

Sweet potato and coconut soup

This rich, filling soup is ideal for a weekend lunch. If you cannot find a whole coconut, instead of the homemade coconut milk, you can use 2½ cups water and a 1¾ cups canned coconut milk instead.

1 Drill holes in the 3 coconut eyes. Pour out the liquid and reserve. Crack the coconut open, prize out the flesh and grate roughly.

2 Put the grated coconut in a heatproof bowl with the measured boiling water and allow to stand for 1 hour. Squeeze and rub the grated coconut into the water, to extract as much of the juice and oil from the flesh as you can. Strain the liquid into a pitcher. Reserve 2 tablespoons of the coconut pulp.

3 Heat the oil in a large, heavy saucepan, add the onions and cook over a moderate heat for 10 minutes. Add the sweet potato and cook for 5 minutes. Add the garlic, ginger, crushed red pepper, reserved coconut water, white coconut milk, reserved coconut pulp, and salt and pepper to taste. Bring to a fast simmer without boiling. Reduce the heat, cover, and simmer for 30–35 minutes until the sweet potato is tender.

4 In a blender or food processor, blend the soup in batches, then transfer it to a clean pan. Gently reheat and serve in warm bowls.

25* PREP

55 COOK

4 SERVES

exotic

1 small **coconut**

4 cups boiling **water**

4 tablespoons **olive oil**

2 **onions**, finely chopped

1 lb **sweet potatoes**, roughly chopped

2 **garlic cloves**, crushed

3 inch piece of fresh **gingerroot**, peeled and finely chopped

¼ teaspoon dried **crushed red pepper**

salt and **pepper**

* Plus 1 hour standing

1 lb waxy **new potatoes**, scrubbed

3 small **leeks**

3 tablespoons **butter**

1 tablespoon **black mustard seeds**

1 **onion**, chopped

1 **garlic clove**, thinly sliced

4 cups **Vegetable Stock** (see page 19)

plenty of **grated nutmeg**

small handful of fresh **cilantro**, roughly chopped

salt and **pepper**

warm **bread**, to serve

10

PREP

20

COOK

4

SERVES

herby

New potato, cilantro, and leek soup

Leek and potato is a favorite combination for soups, but the addition of cilantro gives a new twist. Chop the cilantro at the last minute to keep it as fresh as possible.

1 Halve the potatoes or cut them into ½ inch slices if large. Halve the leeks lengthwise, then cut across into thin shreds.

2 Melt the butter in a large, heavy saucepan, add the mustard seeds, onion, garlic, and potatoes and cook over a moderate heat for 5 minutes. Add the stock and nutmeg and bring just to a boil. Reduce the heat, cover, and simmer gently for 10 minutes or until the potatoes are just tender.

3 Stir in the leeks and cilantro and cook for an additional 5 minutes. Season to taste with salt and pepper and serve with warm bread.

Creamed corn and potato soup

This is a soup for cold winter evenings or when you're feeling a bit under the weather. The comforting combination of potato and corn is guaranteed to cheer you up.

10

PREP

20

COOK

4

SERVES

filling

2 tablespoons **olive oil**

1 **onion**, chopped

2 **celery sticks**, thinly sliced

4 cups **Vegetable Stock** (see page 19)

3 cups diced **potatoes**

1¾ cups frozen **corn kernels**

2 tablespoons chopped **tarragon**

plenty of **grated nutmeg**

4 tablespoons **heavy cream**

salt and **pepper**

1 Heat the oil in a large, heavy saucepan, add the onion and celery and cook over a moderate heat for 5 minutes. Add the stock and bring to a boil.

2 Add the potatoes, then reduce the heat and simmer, uncovered, for 5 minutes. Add the corn kernels and tarragon, cover and simmer for an additional 5 minutes or until the potatoes are tender.

3 In a blender or food processor, blend the soup in batches until pulpy but not smooth, then return it to the pan.

4 Add the nutmeg and cream. Season to taste with salt and pepper. Reheat gently for 1 minute, then serve in warm soup bowls.

¼ cup **butter**

1 small **onion**, chopped

2 **dessert apples**, peeled, cored, and sliced

pinch of **cayenne pepper** (or to taste)

4 cups **Vegetable Stock** (see page 19)

2½ cups sliced **potatoes**

1¼ cups hot **milk**

salt

TO GARNISH:

1 tablespoon **butter**

2–3 thinly sliced **dessert apple** quarters

cayenne pepper

15

PREP

30

COOK

4

SERVES

spicy

Spicy apple and potato soup

The combination of apple and potato is not an obvious one, but this soup is delicious. The cayenne pepper adds spice and contrast to the velvety smooth texture.

1 Melt the butter in a large, heavy saucepan, add the onion and cook over a moderate heat for 5 minutes or until softened. Add the apples and cayenne pepper and cook, stirring, for 2 minutes. Pour in the stock, then add the potatoes. Bring to a boil, then reduce the heat and simmer gently for 15–18 minutes or until the apples and potatoes are very tender.

2 In a blender or food processor, blend the soup in batches until very smooth, then transfer it to a clean saucepan. Reheat gently and stir in the hot milk. Taste and adjust the seasoning if necessary.

3 Meanwhile, make the garnish. Melt the butter in a small skillet, add the apple and cook over a high heat until crisp. Serve the soup in warm bowls, garnishing each portion with some sliced apple and a sprinkling of cayenne pepper.

Cream of celeriac soup

15

PREP

45

COOK

4

SERVES

rich

Creamed soups are always a favorite. Blended vegetables work really well with the addition of milk or cream, and the pinch of freshly grated nutmeg in this recipe finishes the soup off perfectly.

1 Put the stock in a large, heavy saucepan with the bay leaf, nutmeg, and pepper. Bring to a boil.

2 Add the celeriac and potatoes and season to taste with salt. Return to a boil, then reduce the heat, partially cover, and simmer for 35 minutes or until all the vegetables are tender. Remove and discard the bay leaf.

3 In a blender or food processor, blend the soup in batches, then transfer it to a clean saucepan. Reheat gently without boiling and stir in the cream. Ladle into warm soup bowls, sprinkle each portion with finely chopped parsley and serve immediately.

5 cups **Vegetable Stock** (see page 19)

1 **bay leaf**

pinch of **grated nutmeg**

¼ teaspoon **white pepper**

about 1½ lb **celeriac**, diced

3 cups diced **potatoes**

1 cup **light cream**

salt

finely chopped **parsley**, to garnish

¼ cup **unsalted butter**

1 lb **celery**, sliced, leaves reserved to garnish

3 cups chopped **carrots**

8 oz **dessert apples**, peeled, cored, and roughly chopped

5 cups **Vegetable Stock** (see page 19)

1 teaspoon **paprika**, plus extra to garnish

cayenne pepper, to taste

1 tablespoon chopped **basil**

1 **bay leaf**

1 teaspoon grated fresh **gingerroot**

salt and **white pepper**

15

PREP

60

COOK

6

SERVES

tasty

Celery, carrot, and apple soup

This interesting combination of ingredients blends together surprisingly well. The herbs and spices add color, fragrant flavor, and a little heat.

1 Melt the butter in a large, heavy saucepan and add the celery, carrots, and apple. Cover tightly and cook over a low heat, stirring occasionally, for 15 minutes.

2 Add the stock, paprika, cayenne pepper, basil, bay leaf, and ginger. Bring to a boil, then reduce the heat, partially cover, and simmer for about 40–45 minutes until the vegetables and apple are tender.

3 In a blender or food processor, blend the soup in batches until smooth, then transfer it to a bowl. Press through a sieve into a clean saucepan, then season to taste with salt and pepper. Reheat gently. Ladle into warm soup bowls, and serve immediately, garnishing each portion with finely chopped celery leaves and a light sprinkling of paprika.

Cream of celery and leek soup

Cooked celery has quite a strong flavor and tastes quite different from raw celery. It is used here with leeks, and little else is required to flavor the soup.

15

PREP

60

COOK

6

SERVES

thick

1 Melt the butter in a large, heavy saucepan and add the celery and leeks. Cover tightly and cook over a low heat, stirring occasionally, for 15 minutes.

2 Add the stock, parsley, and bay leaf. Bring to a boil, then reduce the heat, partially cover, and simmer for 40–45 minutes. Remove and discard the parsley and bay leaf.

3 In a blender or food processor, blend the soup in batches until smooth, then transfer it to a bowl. Press through a sieve into a clean saucepan, then season to taste with salt and pepper. Reheat gently without boiling. Stir in the cream, then serve immediately in warm soup bowls, garnishing each portion with finely chopped celery leaves.

¼ cup **butter**

1 lb **celery**, sliced, leaves reserved to garnish

8 oz **leeks**, white parts only, sliced

5 cups **Vegetable Stock** (see page 19)

1 sprig of **parsley**

1 **bay leaf**

⅔ cups **heavy cream**

salt and **white pepper**

PESTO:

3 **garlic cloves**, crushed

handful of **basil**

2 tablespoons **pine nuts**

⅔ grated **Parmesan cheese**

3 tablespoons **olive oil**

SOUP:

3 tablespoons **olive oil**

1 **onion**, diced

2 **leeks**, sliced

1 **potato**, chopped

14 oz can **kidney beans**, rinsed and drained

6 cups **Vegetable Stock** (see page 19)

2 **zucchini**, diced

4 oz small **green beans**, cut into small pieces

4 oz **broccoli** florets, chopped

8 oz can **artichoke hearts**

1 tablespoon **flat leaf parsley**, chopped

salt and **pepper**

20

PREP

20

COOK

4

SERVES

fresh

Pesto and vegetable soup

Homemade pesto is easy to make, and you could also use this version as a pasta sauce. The wonderful array of vegetables results in a colorful soup that's packed full of vitamins and minerals. Serve it with warm focaccia bread for a substantial meal.

1 Make the pesto. In a blender or food processor, blend the garlic, basil, pine nuts, and Parmesan thoroughly. Add the oil and blend again. Set aside.

2 Heat the oil for the soup in a large, heavy saucepan, add the onion and leeks and cook over a moderate heat for 3 minutes.

3 Add the potato, beans, and stock and season with salt and pepper. Bring to a boil, then reduce the heat and simmer for 12 minutes.

4 Add the zucchini, green beans, broccoli, and artichoke hearts to the pan and simmer for 5 minutes.

5 Add the parsley and pesto and stir well. Serve immediately in warm soup bowls.

Chili and pimiento soup

The fresh red chili gives this soup a bit of a punch, and it would be good to serve as an appetizer for a Mexican meal. Serve the soup with some tortilla chips for dunking.

1 Heat the oil in a large, heavy saucepan, add the onions, garlic, and chili and cook over a moderate heat for 3 minutes.

2 Add the pimientos, tomatoes, sugar, and stock and bring to a boil. Reduce the heat, cover, and simmer gently for 10 minutes or until the tomatoes are tender.

3 In a blender or food processor, blend the soup in batches until smooth, then return it to the pan. Stir in the cilantro and crème fraîche, then season to taste with salt and pepper. Reheat gently for 1 minute, then serve in warm soup bowls.

10 PREP

15 COOK

4 SERVES

hot

2 tablespoons **olive oil**

2 **onions**, chopped

2 **garlic cloves**, chopped

1 **red chili**, seeded and sliced

7 oz jar **pimientos**, drained

1 lb **tomatoes**, skinned

2 teaspoons **superfine sugar**

4 cups **Vegetable Stock** (see page 19)

2 tablespoons chopped fresh **cilantro**

4 tablespoons **crème fraîche**

salt and **pepper**

3 tablspoons **ghee** or **butter**

1 **onion**, chopped

2 **garlic cloves**, crushed

2 teaspoons grated fresh **gingerroot**

1 large **potato**, diced

1 large **carrot**, diced

2 teaspoons **ground coriander**

1 teaspoon **ground cumin**

½ teaspoon **garam masala**

½ cup **red lentils**, washed and drained

2½ cups **Vegetable Stock** (see page 19)

2½ cups **tomato juice**

salt and **pepper**

TO SERVE:

raita

naan bread

15

PREP

35

COOK

4

SERVES

hearty

Curried vegetable soup

This warming and satisfying dish is ideal for cold winter nights. Ghee, traditionally used in Indian cooking for pan-frying, is rather similar to clarified butter. You can find it in cans in some gourmet markets or seek it out in a specialist Indian food store.

1 Melt the ghee or butter in a large, heavy saucepan, add the onion, garlic, ginger, potato, and carrot and cook over a moderate heat for 10 minutes. Stir in the spices and then add all the remaining ingredients.

2 Bring to a boil, then reduce the heat, cover, and simmer gently for 20–25 minutes or until the lentils and vegetables are tender.

3 Season to taste with salt and pepper, then spoon the soup into warm bowls. Top each bowl with a spoonful of raita and serve with naan bread.

Walnut soup

This intense, rich soup, which is made with toasted and ground walnuts, can be found all over the Middle East and also in North Africa, where nuts are widely used in cooking.

15
PREP

25
COOK

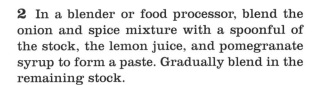

6
SERVES

stylish

1 Heat the oil in a large, heavy saucepan, add the onion, garlic, cinnamon, cumin, and coriander and cook, stirring frequently, for 5 minutes or until lightly golden. Add the walnuts and bread crumbs and cook, stirring occasionally, for an additional 5 minutes.

2 In a blender or food processor, blend the onion and spice mixture with a spoonful of the stock, the lemon juice, and pomegranate syrup to form a paste. Gradually blend in the remaining stock.

3 Return the mixture to the saucepan and bring slowly to a boil. Reduce the heat, cover, and simmer for 15 minutes. Season to taste with salt and pepper. Serve in warm soup bowls topped with a spoonful of yogurt and a drizzle of chili oil.

4 tablespoons **walnut oil** or **olive oil**

1 **onion**, finely chopped

1 **garlic clove**, crushed

1 teaspoon **ground cinnamon**

¼ teaspoon **ground cumin**

¼ teaspoon **ground coriander**

1½ cups **walnuts**, toasted and chopped

½ cup dry **bread crumbs**

4 cups **Vegetable Stock** (see page 19)

1 tablespoon **lemon juice**

1 tablespoon **pomegranate syrup**

salt and **pepper**

TO SERVE:

Greek or whole milk yogurt

chili oil

12 oz **Jerusalem artichokes** or **Chinese artichokes**, scrubbed

2 tablespoons **butter**, melted

1 tablespoon **olive oil**

1 **onion**, finely chopped

1 sprig of **thyme**

2½ cups **Vegetable Stock** (see page 19)

⅔ cup **heavy cream**

salt and **pepper**

large thick bread **croutons**, to serve

SALSA DULCE:

1 **garlic clove**

¼ cups dry **bread crumbs**

1 tablespoon chopped **flat leaf parsley**

1 tablespoon chopped **dill**

1 tablespoon chopped **tarragon**

1 small **red bell pepper**, cored, seeded, and finely chopped

3 tablespoons **olive oil**

15

PREP

50

COOK

4

SERVES

exotic

Roasted artichoke soup

You can use Jerusalem or Chinese artichokes in this soup. Roasting them contributes a slightly smoky flavor to the soup, while the salsa dulce, made with green herbs and sweet red pepper, adds a dash of color and a punch of aroma. The salsa is stirred into the soup just before eating.

1 Cut the Jerusalem artichokes in half if they are large. Put in a small roasting pan and drizzle over the melted butter. Sprinkle with salt and pepper to taste. Roast in a preheated oven, 400°F, for 30 minutes (10 minutes for Chinese artichokes) or until cooked through and lightly browned.

2 Heat the oil in a large, heavy saucepan, add the onion and cook over a moderate heat for 5 minutes. Add the roasted artichokes, thyme, and stock and bring to a gentle boil. Reduce the heat and simmer for 10 minutes. Add salt and pepper to taste.

3 Meanwhile, make the salsa. In a blender or food processor, blend the garlic, bread crumbs, and herbs until finely chopped. Add the red pepper, oil, and salt and pepper to taste and blend to a coarse puree. Set aside.

4 In the blender or food processor, blend the soup in batches until smooth, then return it to the pan. Reheat gently, then add the cream. Serve in warm soup bowls, each serving topped with a crouton and a spoonful of salsa.

Jerusalem artichoke soup

15

PREP

40

COOK

6

SERVES

rich

2 lb **Jerusalem artichokes**

lemon juice

¼ cup **butter**

1 **onion**, chopped

2½ cups **Vegetable Stock** (see page 19)

2½ cups **milk**

⅔ cup **light cream**

salt and **white pepper**

TO GARNISH:

finely chopped **parsley**

croutons

The Jerusalem artichoke received its name through inaccurate description and incorrect pronunciation, since it has nothing to do with an artichoke or with Jerusalem. These tubers were originally grown by Native Americans and were discovered in 1605 by French explorers in Massachusetts.

1 If the artichokes are fairly smooth, peel and drop immediately into acidulated water (with lemon juice) to prevent discoloration. If they are knobbly, scrub in plenty of water and cut off the dark tips and any small, dry roots. Slice the artichokes and drop immediately into acidulated water.

2 Melt the butter in a large, heavy saucepan, add the onion and cook over a moderate heat for 5 minutes or until softened. Add the artichokes and cook, stirring, for 3 minutes. Season to taste with salt and pepper. Add the stock and milk. Bring to simmering point, stirring constantly. Reduce the heat, partially cover, and simmer for 30 minutes or until the vegetables are tender.

3 In a blender or food processor, blend the soup briefly in batches, then transfer it to a clean saucepan. Reheat gently without boiling, then add the cream. Serve in warm soup bowls, garnished with finely chopped parsley and croutons.

¼ cup **butter**

1 **onion**, chopped

1 **garlic clove**, chopped

1 **celery stick**, sliced

14 oz can **artichoke hearts**, drained

5 cups **Vegetable Stock** (see page 19)

1 tablespoon **lemon juice**

3 tablespoons chopped **dill**

2 tablespoons **all-purpose flour**

⅔ cup **light cream**

salt and **white pepper**

4–6 sprigs of **dill**, to garnish

20

PREP

35

COOK

4

SERVES

posh

Heart of artichoke soup with dill

Dill has a distinctive taste, and is often used with fish, such as salmon. Here, it works well with the tender artichoke hearts. This is a good soup for entertaining.

1 Melt the butter in a large, heavy saucepan and add the onion, garlic, and celery. Cover and cook over a moderate heat, stirring occasionally, for 10–12 minutes or until all the vegetables are tender.

2 Add the artichoke hearts, cover, and cook for an additional 3 minutes. Pour in 4 cups of the stock and the lemon juice. Stir in 1 tablespoon of the dill. Cover and simmer for about 15 minutes.

3 In a blender or food processor, blend the soup in batches until smooth, transferring to a clean saucepan.

4 In a small bowl, blend the flour with the remaining stock, adding a little water if necessary. Reheat the soup, beat in the flour mixture and cook, stirring constantly, until slightly thickened. Add the remaining dill and season to taste with salt and pepper, then add the cream. Heat thoroughly without boiling. Serve the soup in warm soup bowls, garnishing each portion with a dill sprig.

Watercress and apple soup

15

PREP

30

COOK

4

SERVES

light

Watercress is usually confined to salads, but it makes a really good soup, especially when it's combined with cream. Dessert apples don't have to be too sweet and are ideal for savory dishes.

1 Melt the butter in a large, heavy saucepan, add the watercress and apples and cook over a moderate heat for 3–5 minutes. Stir in the stock, potatoes, lemon juice, and nutmeg and season to taste with salt and pepper. Bring to a boil, then reduce the heat, cover, and simmer for 15–20 minutes or until the apples and potatoes are tender.

2 In a blender or food processor, blend the soup in batches until smooth, then transfer it to a clean saucepan. Add the cream and gently reheat without boiling. Serve the soup in warm soup bowls, garnishing each portion with a sprinkling of the finely chopped apple.

¼ cup **butter**

2 bunches of **watercress**, stalks discarded, roughly chopped

4 oz peeled, cored, and chopped **dessert apples**

4 cups **Vegetable Stock** (see page 19)

2 cups chopped **potatoes**

1 teaspoon **lemon juice**

pinch of **grated nutmeg**

⅔ cup **light cream**, chilled

salt and **pepper**

1 tablespoon finely chopped **dessert apple**, to garnish

¼ cup **butter**

1 **onion**, chopped

1 **celery stick**, sliced

1 large **cauliflower**, about 1½ lb, cut into small florets

2½ cups **Vegetable Stock** (see page 19)

4 cups **milk**

1 teaspoon **grated nutmeg**

1 tablespoon **cornstarch**

8 oz **Stilton cheese**, crumbled

½ cup **heavy cream**

salt and **white pepper**

finely chopped **parsley**, to garnish

PREP
15

COOK
35

SERVES
6

filling

Cauliflower soup with Stilton

Cauliflower is a versatile vegetable that can be transformed into a variety of flavorsome soups. Cheese is a delicious accompaniment.

1 Melt the butter in a large, heavy saucepan and add the onion, celery, and cauliflower. Cover and cook over a moderate heat, stirring frequently, for 5–8 minutes. Stir in the stock with 2 cups of milk. Bring to a boil, reduce the heat, cover, and simmer for 25 minutes.

2 In a blender or food processor, blend the soup in batches until smooth, then transfer it to a clean saucepan. Stir in 1¼ cups of the remaining milk. Season to taste with salt and pepper and stir in the nutmeg.

3 In a small bowl, blend the cornstarch with the remaining milk and add to the soup. Bring to a boil, stirring constantly. Reduce the heat and simmer for 2 minutes. Stir in the Stilton and cream. Heat through gently without boiling, stirring constantly. Serve immediately in warm soup bowls, garnished with a sprinkling of finely chopped parsley.

Carrot soup

The humble, versatile carrot with its bright color and sweetish flavor can be used in a variety of delicious soups.

15 PREP

40 COOK

6 SERVES

simple

¼ cup **butter**

1 **onion**, chopped

1 lb **carrots**, sliced

2 **turnips**, diced

4 cups **water**

2½ cups **Vegetable Stock** (see page 19)

2 cups sliced **potatoes**

pinch of **superfine sugar**

3 tablespoons **heavy cream** (optional)

salt and **pepper**

1 Melt the butter in a large, heavy saucepan, add the onion and cook over a moderate heat for 5 minutes or until softened. Add the carrots and turnips and cook, stirring all the time, for 1 minute. Pour in the measured water and the stock. Stir, then add the potatoes and sugar. Season to taste with salt and pepper. Bring to a boil. Reduce the heat, cover, and simmer for 25–30 minutes.

2 In a blender or food processor, blend the soup in batches until smooth, then transfer it to a clean saucepan.

3 Reheat gently without boiling. Taste and adjust the seasoning if necessary. Just before serving, stir in the cream, if desired. Serve in warm soup bowls.

¼ cup **butter**

1 **onion**, chopped

1 lb **carrots**, sliced

2 **turnips**, diced

4 cups **water**

2½ cups **Vegetable Stock**
(see page 19)

2 cups sliced **potatoes**

pinch of **superfine sugar**

2–3 tablespoons mild
curry powder

½ teaspoon **ground
cumin**

½ teaspoon **ground
turmeric**

⅔ cup **heavy cream**

salt and **pepper**

15

PREP

40

COOK

6

SERVES

spicy

Creamy curried carrot soup

This is an easy-to-cook variation of the basic Carrot Soup (see page 141). It's ideal for a quick midweek supper and delicious served with warm crusty bread or naan bread.

1 Melt the butter in a large, heavy saucepan, add the onion and cook over a moderate heat for 5 minutes until softened. Add the carrots and turnips and cook, stirring constantly, for 1 minute. Pour in the measured water and the stock. Stir, then add the potatoes and sugar. Season to taste with salt and pepper. Add the curry powder, cumin and turmeric. Bring to a boil. Reduce the heat, cover, and simmer for 25–30 minutes.

2 In a blender or food processor, blend the soup in batches until smooth, then transfer it to a clean saucepan.

3 Add the cream and reheat gently without boiling. Taste and adjust the seasoning if necessary. Serve in warm soup bowls.

Cream of asparagus soup

Save this recipe for when fresh asparagus is in season. This is a simple soup that relies on the quality of its ingredients to make it shine.

10

PREP

30

COOK

6

SERVES

classic

2 lb **asparagus**

8 cups **water**

2 tablespoons **butter**

1 tablespoon **all-purpose flour**

pinch of **grated nutmeg**

2 **egg yolks**

1¼ cups **heavy cream**

salt and **white pepper**

1 tablespoon snipped **chives**, to garnish

1 Trim the ends of the asparagus and cut the spears into 1 inch segments. Bring the measured water, lightly salted, to a boil, add the asparagus and cook for 15 minutes or until very tender. Drain, reserving the liquid in a pitcher.

2 Melt the butter in a large, heavy saucepan, stir in the flour and cook over a moderate heat, stirring constantly, for 1 minute. Gradually add the reserved liquid, bring to a boil, stirring constantly, and cook until thickened. Add the nutmeg and salt and pepper to taste and cook, stirring frequently, for an additional 3–5 minutes.

3 Add the asparagus and reduce the heat. Simmer gently, stirring occasionally, for an additional 5 minutes.

4 In a small bowl, beat the egg yolks with the cream and add a little pepper. Pour into the soup. Stir well and cook for an additional 1 minute without boiling. Serve in warm soup bowls, garnishing each portion with a sprinkling of snipped chives.

1 tablespoon **olive oil**

2 oz rindless **bacon**, finely chopped

1 **onion**, chopped

1 **celery stick**, thinly sliced

12 oz **Brussels sprouts**, trimmed and chopped

4 cups **water**

12 oz **potatoes**, cut into ½ inch cubes

1 teaspoon finely chopped **marjoram**

pinch of **grated nutmeg** (or to taste)

1 **egg yolk**

4 tablespoons **milk**

salt and **white pepper**

15

PREP

50

COOK

6

SERVES

hearty

Brussels sprouts soup

Brussels sprouts don't tend to feature on many people's list of favorite vegetables, and this is a great way to disguise them! Once people have complimented you on the soup, they might change their minds.

1 Heat the oil in a large, heavy saucepan, add the bacon and cook over a moderate heat for 5 minutes or until golden. Add the onion and celery, cover, and cook, stirring quite frequently, for 5 minutes. Add the Brussels sprouts and cook for 5–8 minutes.

2 Stir in the measured water, potatoes, marjoram, and nutmeg and bring to a boil. Reduce the heat and simmer, uncovered, for 30 minutes or until the potatoes are tender. Season to taste with salt and pepper.

3 In a blender or food processor, blend the soup in batches until smooth, then transfer it to a clean saucepan.

4 In a small bowl, beat the egg yolk with the milk. Bring the soup to simmering point, then stir in the egg and milk mixture and heat through without boiling. Serve the soup immediately in warm soup bowls.

Kale soup with garlic croutons

Garlic croutons provide a crisp counterpoint to this soup. They can be made in advance and stored in the refrigerator in an airtight container. To reheat, spread the croutons on a baking sheet and place in a very hot oven for a few minutes.

25

PREP

45

COOK

8

SERVES

stylish

¼ cup **butter**

1 **onion**, chopped

2 **carrots**, sliced

1 lb **kale**, stalks discarded

5 cups **water**

2½ cups **Vegetable Stock** (see page 19)

1 tablespoon **lemon juice**

2½ cups sliced **potatoes**

pinch of **grated nutmeg**

salt and **pepper**

2 **kale leaves**, thinly shredded, to garnish

GARLIC CROUTONS:

6–8 tablespoons **olive oil**

3 **garlic cloves**, sliced

6–8 slices of white or brown **bread**, crusts removed, cut into ½ inch squares

1 Melt the butter in a large saucepan, add the onion and cook over a moderate heat for 5 minutes or until softened. Add the carrots and kale in batches, stirring constantly. Cook for 2 minutes. Add the measured water, stock, lemon juice, potatoes, nutmeg, and salt and pepper to taste. Bring to a boil, then reduce the heat, cover, and simmer for 30–35 minutes or until all the vegetables are tender.

2 In a blender or food processor, blend the soup in batches, then transfer it to a clean saucepan. Add a little water if it is too thick.

3 Meanwhile, make the croutons. Heat the oil in a large skillet, add the garlic and cook over a moderate heat for 1 minute. Add the bread and cook, turning frequently, until golden brown. Remove with a slotted spoon and drain on paper towels. Remove and discard the garlic. Add the shredded kale and cook, stirring constantly, until crispy.

4 Reheat the soup gently. Serve in warm soup bowls, garnished with the croutons and crispy kale.

Greens soup

1 lb **kale**, stalks discarded

1 lb **greens**, stalks discarded, roughly chopped

8 oz **leeks**, sliced

1 teaspoon **caraway seeds**

3 **garlic cloves**, crushed

1 tablespoon **olive oil**

7 cups **water**

⅔ cup **dry white wine**

½ cup **ricotta cheese**

½ cup **crème fraîche**

½ cup **plain yogurt**

salt and **white pepper**

20

PREP

75

COOK

6

SERVES

simple

What a great way to eat your greens! This soup is full to bursting with healthy, tasty vegetables. The rather coarse texture gives it a rustic feel, and the color is fantastic.

1 Mix the kale, greens, leeks, caraway seeds, garlic, and oil in a large, heavy saucepan. Add the measured water, partially cover, and bring to a boil. Reduce the heat and simmer for 45 minutes.

2 Drain the vegetables through a colander or sieve, reserving the liquid. In a blender or food processor, blend the vegetables until finely chopped but not pureed.

3 In a large, clean saucepan, combine 2½ cups of the reserved liquid with the wine. Cook over a low heat for 3 minutes, then beat in the ricotta cheese, crème fraîche and yogurt. Stir well and simmer for an additional 3 minutes. Add the finely chopped vegetables. Stir in most of the remaining liquid to make a fairly thick soup.

4 Partially cover and simmer gently without boiling, stirring occasionally, for 20 minutes. Season to taste with salt and pepper. Serve immediately in warm soup bowls.

Parsley soup

PREP 10

COOK 55

In this soup recipe, parsley is used more as a vegetable than a herb. With its wonderful, fresh flavor, it's a shame to bring it out only for garnishes, and this soup proves it should be used more often.

5 oz **parsley**, plus extra leaves to garnish

2½ cups **water**

2 tablespoons **butter**

1 **onion**, finely chopped

14 oz **potatoes**, cut into ½ inch strips

¼ teaspoon **grated nutmeg**

salt and **white pepper**

1 Put the parsley and measured water in a saucepan and bring to a boil, then reduce the heat, cover, and simmer for 30 minutes.

2 Rub the mixture through a sieve set over a large bowl. Discard the parsley remaining in the sieve.

3 Melt the butter in a large, heavy saucepan, add the onion and cook over a moderate heat for 5 minutes or until softened. Add the parsley liquid and potatoes and bring to a boil, reduce the heat, cover, and simmer for about 15–20 minutes until the potatoes are tender.

4 Add the nutmeg and salt and pepper to taste. Serve the soup in warm soup bowls, garnishing each portion with parsley leaves.

SERVES 4

herby

1/4 cup **butter**

1 **garlic clove**, crushed

1 **onion**, chopped

1 tablespoon mild **curry powder**

6 cups **Vegetable Stock** (see page 19)

1 teaspoon chopped **marjoram**

1 **bay leaf**

1 lb **green beans**, cut into 1/2 inch pieces

2–2 1/2 cups diced **potatoes**

salt

2/3 cup **sour cream**, to garnish

15

PREP

55

COOK

6

SERVES

spicy

Curried green bean soup

Sour cream is the perfect garnish for spicy soups. It's important to add it to the bowls just before serving, because it will begin to melt into the soup immediately. The cool, almost tart, flavor will cut through the heat of the soup.

1 Melt the butter in a large, heavy saucepan, add the garlic and onion and cook over a moderate heat for 5 minutes or until softened but not browned. Stir in the curry powder and cook, stirring, for 2 minutes.

2 Pour in the stock and add the marjoram, bay leaf, beans, and potatoes. Season to taste with salt. Bring to a boil, then reduce the heat, cover, and simmer for 45 minutes or until the vegetables are tender. Remove and discard the bay leaf.

3 In a blender or food processor, blend the soup in batches until smooth, then return it to the saucepan. Reheat gently without boiling. Serve in warm soup bowls, garnishing each portion with a swirl of sour cream.

Cheddar cheese soup

Buy good-quality cheese to ensure that the soup has a rich flavor. Vintage varieties will obviously be stronger, so choose according to your personal taste.

10

PREP

15

COOK

6

SERVES

quick

¼ cup **butter**

1 **onion**, finely grated

¼ cup **all-purpose flour**

4 cups **Chicken Stock** (see page 17)

2 cups **milk**

8 oz **cheddar cheese**, grated

½ teaspoon **white pepper**

salt

1 Melt the butter in a large, heavy saucepan, add the onion and cook over a moderate heat for 5 minutes or until softened. Sprinkle in the flour and stir until well blended. Gradually add the warm stock, stirring constantly. Bring to a boil and cook, stirring constantly, until thickened.

2 Reduce the heat and stir in the milk, cheese, and pepper. Season to taste with salt. Cook over a low heat, stirring constantly, until the cheese has melted and the soup begins to bubble. Serve immediately in warm soup bowls.

hearty

4 tablespoons extra virgin **olive oil**

1 large **onion**, chopped

2 oz **chorizo sausage**, chopped

4 **garlic cloves**, crushed

2 tablespoons chopped **thyme**

5 cups **passata** (pureed tomatoes)

3 cups **Chicken Stock** (see page 17)

2 x 13 oz cans **cranberry beans**, rinsed and drained

7 oz **conchigliette** or other small pasta shapes

3 tablespoons chopped **basil**

salt and **pepper**

grated **Parmesan cheese**, to serve

15
PREP

35
COOK

6
SERVES

feast

Chunky chorizo, pasta, and bean soup

This substantial winter soup is based on the Italian classic **pasta e fagioli** (pasta and beans). Pieces of fiery chorizo sausage add a lovely spiciness to the dish. The tiny pasta shapes used for soup are known as pastina, and there are dozens of different types to choose from.

1 Heat the oil in a large, heavy saucepan, add the onion, chorizo, garlic, and thyme and cook over a moderate heat for 5 minutes. Add the passata, stock, and beans. Season to taste with salt and pepper and bring to a boil, then reduce the heat, cover, and simmer for about 20 minutes.

2 Stir in the pasta and basil and simmer for an additional 8–10 minutes or until the pasta is tender. Taste and adjust the seasoning if necessary. Ladle into warm bowls and serve topped with grated Parmesan.

Pumpkin soup with crusty cheese topping

25
PREP

60
COOK

If you prefer to make croutons, broil the baguette slices on one side, then turn them over, top with the cheese and replace under the broiler until the cheese begins to melt. They can be used to garnish many different flavored soups.

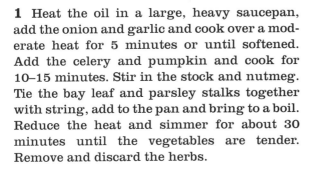

1 Heat the oil in a large, heavy saucepan, add the onion and garlic and cook over a moderate heat for 5 minutes or until softened. Add the celery and pumpkin and cook for 10–15 minutes. Stir in the stock and nutmeg. Tie the bay leaf and parsley stalks together with string, add to the pan and bring to a boil. Reduce the heat and simmer for about 30 minutes until the vegetables are tender. Remove and discard the herbs.

2 In a blender or food processor, blend the soup in batches until smooth, then return it to the pan. Bring to a boil and season with salt and pepper. Stir in the cream and parsley and reheat gently without boiling.

3 Meanwhile, put the bread slices for the garnish on a baking sheet. Toast under a preheated hot broiler until golden on both sides.

4 Pour the soup into 4 deep ovenproof bowls. Arrange 2 toast slices, overlapping, on each. Sprinkle with the cheese. Put on the baking sheet. Cook under the broiler until the cheese is browned and bubbling. Serve immediately.

4
SERVES

rich

1½ tablespoons **olive oil**

1 large **onion**, finely chopped

3 **garlic cloves**, crushed

2 **celery sticks**, chopped

1½ lb **pumpkin** flesh, roughly chopped

4 cups **Vegetable Stock** (see page 19)

pinch of **grated nutmeg**

1 **bay leaf**

few **parsley** stalks

⅓ cup **light cream**

1–2 tablespoons finely chopped **parsley**

salt and **pepper**

TO GARNISH:

1 small **baguette**, cut into 8 slices

2 oz **Gruyère cheese**, grated

6–8 **garlic cloves**, unpeeled

3 tablespoons **olive oil**

1 large **onion**, chopped

2 **celery sticks**, chopped

1 **leek**, chopped

6 **allspice berries**, crushed

1 sprig of **thyme**

1 **bay leaf**

2 **tomatoes**, skinned and chopped

3 tablespoons **peanut butter**

1½ lb **pumpkin**, peeled and cubed

6 cups **Vegetable Stock** (see page 19)

salt and **pepper**

TO SERVE:

¾ cup **sour cream** or **crème fraîche**

breadsticks (optional)

20

PREP

60

COOK

4

SERVES

tasty

Pumpkin and peanut butter soup

This unusual recipe includes peanut butter, which adds a creamy, nutty contrast to the pumpkin. Allspice, thyme, and bay round off the soup.

1 Put the garlic cloves in a small roasting pan and toss with 1 tablespoon of the oil. Roast in a preheated oven, 350°F, for 15–20 minutes until softened. Leave until the garlic is cool enough to handle, then pop the cloves out of their skins and reserve.

2 Heat the remaining oil in a large, heavy-saucepan, add the onion, celery, and leek and cook over a moderate heat for 8–10 minutes or until softened. Add the roasted garlic and all of the remaining ingredients and bring to a boil. Reduce the heat and simmer, uncovered, for about 20–30 minutes or until the vegetables are tender.

3 In a blender or food processor, blend the soup in batches until smooth. Strain through a sieve into the pan. Reheat thoroughly. Serve the soup in warm soup bowls, topped with a spoonful of sour cream or crème fraîche and accompanied by breadsticks, if desired.

Chunky carrot and lentil soup

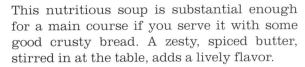

PREP 10

This nutritious soup is substantial enough for a main course if you serve it with some good crusty bread. A zesty, spiced butter, stirred in at the table, adds a lively flavor.

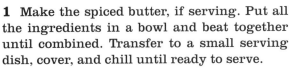

COOK 35

1 Make the spiced butter, if serving. Put all the ingredients in a bowl and beat together until combined. Transfer to a small serving dish, cover, and chill until ready to serve.

2 Heat the oil in a large, heavy saucepan, add the onion and celery and cook over a moderate heat for 5 minutes or until softened. Add the carrots and garlic and cook, stirring, for 3 minutes. Add the lentils and stock and bring just to a boil. Reduce the heat, cover, and simmer for 20–25 minutes until the vegetables are tender and the soup is pulpy. Season to taste with salt and pepper.

3 Ladle the soup into warm bowls and serve the spiced butter (if using) at the table, so that diners can stir in as much as they like.

SERVES 4

spicy

2 tablespoons **vegetable oil**

1 large **onion**, chopped

2 **celery sticks**, sliced

1 lb **carrots**, sliced

1 **garlic clove**, crushed

⅔ cup **split red lentils**, washed and drained

5¾ cups **Vegetable Stock** (see page 19)

salt and **pepper**

SPICED BUTTER (OPTIONAL):

3 tablespoons **lightly salted butter**, softened

2 **scallions**, finely chopped

¼ teaspoon **crushed red pepper**

1 teaspoon **cumin seeds**, lightly crushed

finely grated zest of 1 **lemon**

small handful of fresh **cilantro**, chopped

several sprigs of **mint**, chopped

1 tablespoon **olive oil**

1 **onion**, chopped

2 **carrots**, diced

1 **red bell pepper**, cored, seeded, and diced

2 **garlic cloves**, chopped (optional)

1 small **red chili**, seeded, and chopped

1 teaspoon **cumin seeds**

13 oz can **red kidney beans**, drained and rinsed

1 lb carton **creamed tomatoes** or 2 cups **pureed tomatoes**

2½ cups **Vegetable Stock** (see page 19)

1 tablespoon **brown sugar**

salt and **pepper**

TO GARNISH:

Greek or whole milk yogurt

paprika

cumin seeds

15

PREP

40

COOK

4

SERVES

thick

Chunky chili bean and carrot soup

This warming soup has just a hint of chili. It is made with ingredients that you are likely to have in store, so it makes a good standby for days when you haven't time to shop. If you don't have a bell pepper, you could add an extra carrot.

1 Heat the oil in a large, heavy saucepan, add the onion and cook over a moderate heat for 5 minutes or until softened. Add the carrots, bell pepper, and garlic (if using) and cook, stirring, for 3 minutes or until softened. Stir in the chili and cumin and cook, stirring, for 1 minute.

2 Add the beans, tomatoes, stock, and sugar and season to taste with salt and pepper. Bring to a boil, then reduce the heat, cover, and simmer for 30 minutes or until reduced and thickened.

3 Ladle the soup into bowls and serve topped with a spoonful of yogurt and a sprinkling of paprika and cumin seeds.

Carrot soup with orange and ginger

Carrots team well with garlic and ginger in this tasty soup, and the fresh orange juice provides an unexpected flavor as well as intensifying the color. This soup can also be served lukewarm or cold if you prefer.

10 PREP

20 COOK

6 SERVES

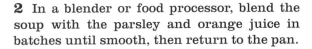

fresh

1½ lb **carrots**, roughly chopped

2 inch piece of fresh **gingerroot**, peeled and finely chopped

4 cups **Vegetable Stock** (see page 19) or **water**

2 tablespoons chopped **parsley**

⅔ cup **orange juice**

salt and **pepper**

buttermilk or **plain yogurt**, to serve

1 Put the carrots in a large, heavy saucepan with the ginger and stock or water and bring to a boil. Reduce the heat and simmer for 12–15 minutes or until the carrots are tender.

2 In a blender or food processor, blend the soup with the parsley and orange juice in batches until smooth, then return to the pan.

3 Season to taste with salt and pepper. Reheat gently, then serve the soup in warm soup bowls with a little buttermilk or yogurt swirled on top.

2 tablespoons **olive oil**

1 large **onion**, chopped

1–2 **garlic cloves**, crushed

1 tablespoon finely grated fresh **gingerroot**

2½ cups sliced **carrots**

4 cups **Vegetable Stock** (see page 19)

2 tablespoons **lime juice** or **lemon juice**

salt and **pepper**

TO SERVE:

sour cream

2 **scallions**, finely chopped

15

PREP

30

COOK

4

SERVES

tasty

Carrot and ginger soup

Carrots have a naturally sweet flavor that works well with ginger. This is a good winter soup—ginger is believed to have many health benefits, which include helping to fight off colds and flu.

1 Heat the oil in a large, heavy saucepan, add the onion, garlic, and ginger and cook over a moderate heat for about 5 minutes or until softened.

2 Add the carrots and stock and bring to a boil. Reduce the heat and simmer for 15–20 minutes or until the carrots are tender.

3 In a blender or food processor, blend the soup with the lime or lemon juice in batches until smooth. Strain through a sieve into the pan. Reheat gently, then serve the soup in warm soup bowls with a spoonful of sour cream and sprinkled with chopped scallions.

Tomato chowder

This is a fantastic stand-by recipe because it can be made from pantry ingredients. It's also very quick to prepare, so there are no excuses for not making your own soup!

1 Mix together all the ingredients except the cheese in a large, heavy saucepan. Bring slowly to a boil, stirring constantly, reduce the heat and simmer, uncovered, for about 3 minutes.

2 Ladle the soup into warm ovenproof bowls and sprinkle with the cheese. Put on a baking sheet and cook under a preheated hot broiler for 3–5 minutes or until the cheese is browned and bubbling. Serve immediately.

5

PREP

12

COOK

4

SERVES

quick

10 oz can **condensed tomato soup**

13 oz can **tomatoes**, sieved

11 oz can **corn kernels**, drained

1 tablespoon **Worcestershire sauce**

3–6 drops of **Tabasco sauce**

1 teaspoon chopped **oregano**

½ teaspoon **superfine sugar**

4 oz **cheddar cheese**, grated

1 tablespoon **olive oil**

1 **onion**, finely chopped

13 oz can **plum tomatoes**

½ teaspoon **superfine sugar**

1¼ cups **Chicken Stock** (see page 17)

2 tablespoons **tomato paste**

2 oz small **pasta shapes**

3 oz frozen **fava beans**

1½ oz **cheddar cheese** or **Gruyère cheese**, crumbled

salt and **pepper**

5

PREP

20

COOK

2

SERVES

easy

Tomato, fava bean, and pasta soup

Canned tomatoes and tiny soup pasta are the main ingredients in this warm and comforting, minestrone-style soup. Served topped with crumbled cheese, it is delicious when accompanied by lightly toasted grainy bread.

1 Heat the oil in a large, heavy saucepan, add the onion and cook over a moderate heat for 5 minutes or until softened. Add the tomatoes, sugar, stock, and tomato paste and bring to a boil. Reduce the heat, cover, and simmer for 5 minutes. Add the pasta, cover, and cook for 5 minutes or until the pasta is tender.

2 Stir in the beans and salt and pepper to taste. Simmer for an additional 2 minutes or until the beans are tender. Ladle into warm soup bowls and serve sprinkled with cheese.

Roasted tomato and chili soup

The combination of tomato and chili is used in many dishes, from curries to pasta sauces, and with good reason. The black olives add a salty contrast to the sweet tomatoes and hot chilies, while lime adds the sour element, making this a perfect dish for the taste buds.

1 Lightly grease a baking sheet with a little of the oil, lay the tomatoes on top, cut side up, and sprinkle with 4 tablespoons of the oil, the salt, and sugar. Add the chili and roast in a preheated oven, 350°, for 45–50 minutes. Remove the chili after 20 minutes. Leave to cool, then peel off the skin, seed, and chop the flesh roughly.

2 Meanwhile, make the olive cream. Fold the olives into the crème fraîche.

3 Heat the remaining oil in a large, heavy saucepan, add the onion and cook over a moderate heat until golden. Add the garlic and cook, stirring, for 2 minutes. Add the roasted tomatoes, the reserved juice and seeds, chili and measured water. Bring to a boil. Reduce the heat and simmer for 10–12 minutes. Season to taste with salt and pepper.

4 In a blender or food processor, blend the soup in batches until smooth. Strain through a fine sieve into the pan. Add lime juice and reheat. Serve in warm soup bowls with a spoonful of the olive cream in each portion.

20
PREP

70
COOK

4
SERVES

hot

3 lb ripe **tomatoes**, preferably plum, seeded and juice and seeds reserved

6 tablespoons extra virgin **olive oil**

1½ teaspoons **sea salt**

1 tablespoon **superfine sugar**

1 large **red chili**

1 **onion**, chopped

1 **garlic clove**, crushed

2½ cups **water**

2–4 tablespoons **lime juice**

salt and **pepper**

OLIVE CREAM:

⅓ cup pitted **black olives**, finely chopped

3 tablespoons **crème fraîche**

1 tablespoon **sunflower** oil

1 **onion**, finely chopped

1 tablespoon **butter**

2 **carrots**, about 8 oz in total, diced

1 **potato**, about 8 oz, diced

1 **parsnip**, about 8 oz, diced

½ teaspoon **ground turmeric**

3 teaspoons mild **curry paste**

5 cups **Vegetable Stock** (see page 19)

⅓ cup **red lentils**, washed and drained

salt and **pepper**

chopped **parsley**, to garnish

15

PREP

55

COOK

4

SERVES

filling

Vegetable and lentil hotpot

This budget-priced soup is a good way to use up the oddments from the vegetable rack and is tasty without being too spicy. It would make a great low-calorie lunch.

1 Heat the oil in a large, heavy saucepan, add the onion and cook over a moderate heat for 5 minutes or until softened. Add the butter and the diced vegetables and cook, stirring frequently, for 5 minutes.

2 Stir in the turmeric and curry paste and cook, stirring, for 1 minute. Add the stock and lentils, then season to taste with salt and pepper. Bring to a boil, then reduce the heat, cover, and simmer for 40 minutes or until the lentils are tender.

3 Ladle into warm soup bowls and serve sprinkled with chopped parsley.

Curried lentil soup

15

PREP

45

COOK

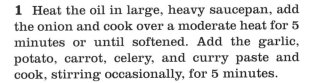

4

SERVES

spicy

Unlike some dried legumes, red, Puy, and continental lentils do not need soaking before use. If you don't have one of the vegetables listed, replace it with something you do have, such as a little diced rutabaga, some butternut squash, a zucchini, or some tomatoes.

1 Heat the oil in large, heavy saucepan, add the onion and cook over a moderate heat for 5 minutes or until softened. Add the garlic, potato, carrot, celery, and curry paste and cook, stirring occasionally, for 5 minutes.

2 Add the lentils, tomatoes, stock, and salt and pepper to taste. Bring to a boil, then reduce the heat, cover, and simmer for 30 minutes or until the lentils are tender.

3 Ladle into warm soup bowls and serve sprinkled with chopped cilantro.

1 tablespoon **vegetable oil**

1 small **onion**, finely chopped

1 **garlic clove**, crushed

1 small **potato**, finely diced

1 **carrot**, finely diced

2 **celery sticks**, finely chopped

1 tablespoon mild **curry paste**

¼ cup **red lentils**, washed and drained

7 oz can chopped **tomatoes**

2½ cups **Chicken Stock** (see page 17)

salt and **pepper**

chopped fresh **cilantro**, to garnish

1 tablespoon **vegetable oil**

1 large **onion**, chopped

2 **garlic cloves**, chopped

1 small **green chili**, seeded and finely chopped (optional)

1 cup **red lentils**, washed and drained

1 **bay leaf**

3 **celery sticks**, thinly sliced

3 **carrots**, thinly sliced

1 **leek**, thinly sliced

6 cups **Vegetable Stock** (see page 19)

13 oz can chopped **tomatoes**

2 tablespoons **tomato paste**

½ teaspoon **ground turmeric**

½ teaspoon **ground ginger**

1 tablespoon chopped fresh **cilantro**

pepper

plain yogurt, to garnish

20

PREP

50

COOK

4

SERVES

hot

Spicy lentil and tomato soup

The lentils will break down when they are cooked, thickening the soup as well as adding plenty of flavor. The soup will keep in the refrigerator for up to three days, or you could freeze individual portions.

1 Heat the oil in a large, heavy saucepan, add the onion, garlic, and chili (if using) and cook over a moderate heat for 5 minutes or until softened. Add the lentils, bay leaf, celery, carrots, leek, and stock. Cover and bring to a boil, then reduce the heat and simmer for 30–40 minutes until the lentils are tender. Remove and discard the bay leaf.

2 Stir in the tomatoes, the tomato paste, turmeric, ginger, and the cilantro. Season to taste with pepper.

3 In a blender or food processor, blend the soup in batches until smooth, adding more stock or water if necessary then return it to the pan. Reheat gently. Ladle the soup into warm soup bowls and serve, each portion garnished with a swirl of yogurt.

Armenian onion and lentil soup

This soup is simmered for over an hour to allow the barley and lentils to cook until tender and absorb the flavor of the onion, herbs, and spices.

15

PREP

105

COOK

8

SERVES

tasty

2 tablespoons **pearl barley**

⅔ cup **water**

7½ cups **Beef Stock** (see page 18)

1 lb **onions**, thinly sliced

⅔ cup **green lentils**, washed and drained

1 teaspoon **dried tarragon**

2 teaspoons **paprika**

pinch of **cayenne pepper**

¼ teaspoon **superfine sugar**

3 tablespoons **dry white wine**

salt and **pepper**

TO GARNISH:

2 tablespoons **butter**

3 tablespoons finely chopped mild **onion**

1 Wash the barley in a colander under cold running water. Drain well and tip into a large, heavy saucepan. Pour in the measured water. Bring to a boil, then reduce the heat, partially cover, and simmer, stirring occasionally, for 25–30 minutes or until all the water is absorbed.

2 Add the stock, onions, lentils, tarragon, paprika, cayenne pepper, sugar, and wine. Bring to a boil. Reduce the heat, partially cover, and simmer for about 1¼ hours. Add a little more water if the soup is too thick. Season to taste with salt and pepper.

3 Meanwhile, melt the butter for the garnish in a small skillet. Add the onion and cook over a moderate heat for 5 minutes or until softened and golden.

4 Ladle the soup into warm soup bowls and serve garnished with the chopped onion.

Harira

20
PREP

65
COOK

8
SERVES

exotic

3 lb free-range **chicken**

2–4 tablespoons **olive oil**

1 **onion**, chopped

4 **garlic cloves**, crushed

1 teaspoon grated fresh **gingerroot**

2 teaspoons **paprika**

¼ teaspoon **saffron threads**

2 x 13 oz cans chopped **tomatoes**

4 cups **water**

¾ cup cooked **chickpeas** (from a can)

¼ cup **red lentils**, washed and drained

¼ cup **basmati rice**

4 tablespoons **lemon juice**

2 tablespoons chopped **parsley**

2 tablespoons chopped fresh **cilantro**

1–2 tablespoons **harissa paste** (optional)

salt and **pepper**

toasted **pita bread**, to serve

Harira is eaten throughout North Africa and the Middle East. Made with lamb or chicken and flavored with lemon and tomatoes, the soup would traditionally have been thickened with yeast or flour. It tastes even better the next day when it thickens naturally, as the liquid is absorbed by the rice and lentils.

1 Joint the chicken into 8 pieces. Heat 2 tablespoons oil in a saucepan, add the chicken pieces and cook until browned on all sides. Remove with a slotted spoon.

2 Add more oil to the pan if necessary. Add the onion, garlic, and ginger and cook over a moderate heat for 10 minutes or until golden. Return the chicken to the pan and add all the remaining ingredients, except the herbs and harissa, with salt and pepper to taste. Cover and simmer gently for 45 minutes.

3 Remove the chicken pieces and allow to cool slightly, then gently pull the flesh away from the bones. Return the meat to the soup. Allow the soup to cool completely, then cover and chill overnight.

4 Reheat the soup, then stir in the herbs and harissa (if using). Serve in warm soup bowls with toasted pita bread.

Bean soup with garlic and chili oil

This is a substantial soup from Tuscany. To give it a sophisticated touch, sliced garlic is fried in chili-flavored olive oil, then poured over the soup at the last moment. The beans may take less time to cook, depending on their freshness, so test after 40 minutes.

35*

PREP

80

COOK

6

SERVES

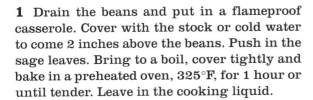

stylish

1¼ cups dried **white beans**, such as kidney or cannellini, soaked overnight in cold water

4 cups **Chicken Stock** (see page 17) or **water**

handful of **sage** leaves

4 **garlic cloves**, 2 finely chopped, 2 thinly sliced

⅔ cup **olive oil**

2 tablespoons chopped **sage** or **rosemary**

good pinch of **crushed red pepper**

salt and **pepper**

1 Drain the beans and put in a flameproof casserole. Cover with the stock or cold water to come 2 inches above the beans. Push in the sage leaves. Bring to a boil, cover tightly and bake in a preheated oven, 325°F, for 1 hour or until tender. Leave in the cooking liquid.

2 In a blender or food processor, blend half of the beans with the sage and all the liquid until smooth. Return to the casserole with the remaining beans. Add more water or stock if the soup is too thick.

3 Heat half of the oil in a nonstick skillet, add the chopped garlic and cook over a moderate heat until golden. Add the herbs and cook for 30 seconds. Stir into the soup and bring to a boil. Reduce the heat and simmer gently for 10 minutes. Season to taste with salt and pepper. Pour into a warm tureen.

4 Cook the sliced garlic in the remaining oil until golden, then stir in the crushed red pepper. Dip the base of the pan into cold water to stop the garlic cooking, then spoon over the soup.

* Plus overnight soaking

3 tablespoons **olive oil**

2 **garlic cloves**, crushed

1 small **red bell pepper**, cored, seeded, and chopped

1 **onion**, finely chopped

¾ cup finely chopped **tomatoes**

1 teaspoon finely chopped **thyme**

½ cup **kidney beans**, soaked overnight in cold water, rinsed, and drained

2½ cups **water**

2½ cups **Vegetable Stock** (see page 19)

2 tablespoons finely chopped **parsley**

salt and **pepper**

15 *

PREP

75

COOK

6

SERVES

posh

White bean soup Provençal

Kidney beans are one of the staples of Mediterranean cuisine, and they make good, thick soups that are ideal for winter evenings. You can use any white bean, such as cannellini, if you have them in store, but adjust the cooking time—the older they are, the longer they take.

1 Heat the oil in a large, heavy saucepan, add the garlic, bell pepper, and onion and cook over a moderate heat for 5 minutes or until softened.

2 Add the tomatoes and thyme and cook for 1 minute. Add the beans and pour in the measured water and stock. Bring to a boil, then reduce the heat, cover, and simmer for 1 hour.

3 Add the parsley and season to taste with salt and pepper. Serve immediately in warm soup bowls.

* Plus overnight soaking

Bean and cabbage soup

Earthy dried beans team perfectly with spicy chorizo and cabbage in this satisfying soup, which makes a complete meal in itself served with hunks of fresh crusty bread.

1 Put the beans in a large, heavy saucepan with 4 oz chorizo in a piece, the rosemary, bouquet garni, and measured water. Bring to a boil and boil rapidly for 10 minutes, then reduce the heat, cover, and simmer gently for 1–1½ hours or until the beans are tender.

2 Meanwhile, heat the oil in a nonstick skillet, add the onion, garlic, bell pepper, and cayenne pepper and cook over a moderate heat for 5 minutes. Dice the remaining chorizo, add to the pan and cook for an additional 5 minutes.

3 Stir the onion mixture into the cooked beans with the cabbage. Season to taste with salt and pepper, bring to a boil and cook for 20 minutes. Add the parsley and taste and adjust the seasoning if necessary. Spoon into warm bowls. Drizzle with olive oil and serve immediately with crusty bread.

20*

PREP

110

COOK

4

SERVES

filling

⅛ cup dried **fava beans**, soaked overnight in cold water, rinsed, and drained

8 oz **chorizo sausage**

2 sprigs of **rosemary**

1 **bouquet garni**

7½ cups cold **water**

2 tablespoons **olive oil**

1 **onion**, chopped

2 **garlic cloves**, crushed

1 small **red bell pepper**, cored, seeded, and chopped

pinch of **cayenne pepper**

2 sups shredded **Savoy cabbage**

1 tablespoon chopped **parsley**

salt and **pepper**

TO SERVE:

olive oil

crusty **bread**

* Plus overnight soaking

WHITE BEAN SOUP:

1¼ cups dried **kidney beans** or **cannellini beans**, soaked overnight in cold water, drained, and rinsed

4 cups **water**

salt and **pepper**

ARUGULA SOUP:

2 tablespoons **butter**

1 **onion**, chopped

2 **potatoes**, about 8 oz in total, cut into ¾ inch dice

3½ cups **arugula**, roughly chopped

1¼ cups **Vegetable Stock** (see page 19)

1¼ cups **milk**

½ cup **heavy cream**

45*

PREP

65

COOK

4

SERVES

party

Arugula and white bean twin soup

This recipe takes a little preparation and a steady hand, but it's well worth the effort. The stark contrast in colors when the two soups are sitting in the bowls really is stunning— save it for special occasions.

1 Make the white bean soup. Put the beans in a saucepan and cover with the measured water. Bring to a boil, then reduce the heat and simmer for 45–60 minutes or until tender. In a blender or food processor, blend the beans and their liquid in batches. Press through a fine sieve into the pan. Season to taste with salt and pepper.

2 Meanwhile, make the arugula soup. Melt the butter in a large, heavy saucepan, add the onion and cook over a moderate heat for 5 minutes or until softened. Add the potatoes, cover, and cook for 5 minutes. Add the arugula, cover, and cook for 3–4 minutes or until wilted. Add the stock, milk, and salt and pepper to taste, then simmer for 10 minutes until the potatoes are tender. In a blender or food processor, blend in batches until smooth. Strain through a sieve into a clean pan.

3 Reheat the 2 soups separately. Add the cream to the arugula soup and heat through. Add more stock or water to the bean soup to make the same consistency. Using 2 ladles, pour the 2 soups simultaneously into bowls.

* Plus overnight soaking

Spanish chickpea soup

15*

PREP

145

COOK

8

SERVES

thick

Known as **garbanzo** in Spain, **ceci** in Italy, and **chana dal** in India, the chickpea is a staple part of the Middle Eastern diet and is used in many European dishes, particularly stews and thick soups like this one.

1 Drain the chickpeas, rinse under cold running water and drain again. Put the ham joint in a large, deep saucepan and cover with cold water. Bring the water briefly to a boil, then drain, discarding the water.

2 Put the ham joint in a large, heavy, clean saucepan. Add the chickpeas, studded onion, garlic, bay leaf, thyme, marjoram, parsley, and measured water. Bring to the boil, then reduce the heat, partially cover, and simmer for 1½ hours. Remove and discard the onion and herbs. Remove the joint, transfer to a board and cut into small pieces. Set aside.

3 Add the stock, potatoes, and cabbage to the pan and simmer for an additional 30 minutes. Add the reserved ham pieces to the soup and cook for an additional 10 minutes. Season to taste with salt and pepper. Serve the soup in warm soup bowls.

1 cup dried **chickpeas**, soaked for 48 hours in cold water or 12 hours in boiling water

1–1½ lb boneless **smoked ham butt joint**

1 **onion**, studded with 4 **cloves**

2 **garlic cloves**, crushed

1 **bay leaf**

1 sprig of **thyme**

1 sprig of **marjoram**

1 sprig of **parsley**

7½ cups **water**

7½ cups **Chicken Stock** (see page 17)

10–12 oz **potatoes**, cut into ½ inch cubes

2½ cups shredded **Savoy cabbage**

salt and **pepper**

* Plus 12–48 hours soaking

¼ cup **butter**

1 **onion**, chopped

1 **garlic clove**, crushed

¼ cup **red lentils**, washed and drained

¼ cup **white long-grain rice**

7½ cups **Vegetable Stock** (see page 19)

1 bunch of **watercress**, stalks discarded, roughly chopped

14 oz can **chickpeas**, drained and rinsed

salt and **pepper**

10

PREP

35

COOK

4

SERVES

easy

Chickpea and watercress soup

This hearty soup is ideal for vegetarians (non-vegetarians could use chicken stock) because it contains protein, carbohydrates, and plenty of vitamins—a meal in a bowl. Serve with whole-wheat bread.

1 Melt the butter in a large, heavy saucepan, add the onion and garlic and cook for 5 minutes or until the onion is softened.

2 Add the lentils and rice and stir well. Pour in the stock and bring to a boil, then reduce the heat, cover, and simmer for 15–18 minutes or until the lentils and rice are tender.

3 Add the watercress and chickpeas. Simmer the soup for an additional 8–10 minutes. Season to taste with salt and pepper and serve in warm soup bowls.

Minestrone soup

Minestrone improves when it is made in advance and reheated. Cover and store in the refrigerator so that the flavors can blend.

1 Heat the oil in a large, heavy saucepan, add the onion, garlic, celery, leek, and carrot and cook over a moderate heat for 3 minutes.

2 Stir in the tomatoes, stock, zucchini, cabbage, bay leaf, and beans. Bring to a boil, then reduce the heat and simmer gently for 10 minutes.

3 Add the spaghetti and season with salt and pepper, then stir well and simmer, stirring frequently, for an additional 8 minutes.

4 Add the parsley and stir well. Ladle into warm soup bowls, scatter with the grated Parmesan, and serve with bruschetta.

20

PREP

25

COOK

4

SERVES

classic

2 tablespoons **olive oil**

1 **onion**, diced

1 **garlic clove**, crushed

2 **celery sticks**, chopped

1 **leek**, thinly sliced

1 **carrot**, chopped

13 oz can chopped **tomatoes**

2½ cups **Vegetable Stock** (see page 19)

1 **zucchini**, diced

½ small **cabbage**, shredded

1 **bay leaf**

3 oz can **kidney beans**, rinsed and drained

3 oz **spaghetti**, broken into small pieces

1 tablespoon chopped **flat leaf parsley**

salt and **pepper**

TO SERVE:

⅔ cup grated **Parmesan cheese**

bruschetta

¼ cup dried **kidney beans**, soaked overnight in cold water

3 tablespoons **olive oil**

2 **garlic cloves**, crushed

1 **celery stick**, chopped

2 **leeks**, sliced

3 **tomatoes**, chopped

3 tablespoons chopped **flat leaf parsley**

2 tablespoons chopped **basil**

4 oz **green beans**, cut into 1 inch pieces

4 oz **asparagus**, cut into 1 inch pieces

4 cups boiling **Vegetable Stock** (see page 19) or **water**

⅓ cup **white long-grain rice**

6 oz **spinach**

1 cup frozen **fava beans**, skinned

1¼ cups frozen **peas**

salt and **pepper**

⅔ cup grated **Parmesan cheese**, to serve

PREP

COOK

SERVES

Minestrone verde

An Italian classic that is a real meal in a bowl. Hearty green vegetables, beans, rice, and plenty of fresh herbs make a soup that's so substantial you won't need bread as well.

1 Drain the kidney beans, rinse under cold running water and drain again. Put in a saucepan and cover with cold water. Bring to a boil, then reduce the heat and simmer for 45–60 minutes or until tender. Remove from the heat and leave in the cooking liquid.

2 Heat the oil in a large, heavy saucepan, add the garlic, celery, and leeks and cook over a moderate heat for 5–10 minutes or until softened. Add the tomatoes with half of the herbs and salt and pepper to taste, then simmer for 12–15 minutes until the tomatoes become pulpy.

3 Add the green beans and asparagus. Cook for 1–2 minutes, then add the stock or water. Bring to a boil and boil rapidly for 10 minutes. Add the rice, cooked kidney beans and their liquid, spinach, fava beans, and peas and cook for 10 minutes. Taste and adjust the seasoning if needed. Ladle into warm bowls and serve the Parmesan separately.

* Plus overnight soaking

Parsnip and orange soup

The humble, inexpensive parsnip can be transformed into a number of delicious soups. The addition of fresh orange imparts a distinctive flavor and color.

15

PREP

45

COOK

6

SERVES

fresh

½ cup **butter**

3 lb **parsnips**, scrubbed and roughly chopped

1 **onion**, chopped

1 **potato**, chopped

grated nutmeg (optional)

⅔ cup freshly squeezed **orange juice**

pared **zest** of 1 **orange**, cut into wide strips

7½ cups **Chicken Stock** (see page 17)

1 teaspoon **lemon juice**

½ cup **heavy cream**

salt and **white pepper**

6–8 **orange segments**, to garnish

1 Melt the butter in a large, heavy saucepan and add the parsnips, onion, potato, and nutmeg (if using). Cover and cook over a low to moderate heat, stirring occasionally, for 10 minutes.

2 Add the orange juice, orange zest strips, and stock. Bring to a boil, then reduce the heat, cover, and simmer for 30 minutes. Remove and discard the orange zest strips.

3 In a blender or food processor, blend the soup in batches until smooth, then transfer it to a clean saucepan. Add a little water if the soup is too thick.

4 Mix the lemon juice with the cream in a pitcher and stir into the soup. Reheat gently without boiling. Season to taste with salt and pepper. Ladle into warm soup bowls and serve immediately, garnishing each portion with an orange segment.

3 tablespoons extra virgin **olive oil**

3 large **red onions**, sliced

1 **fennel bulb**, trimmed and thinly sliced

1 **garlic clove**, crushed

2 tablespoons **red wine vinegar**

1 **bay leaf**

2 sprigs of **thyme**

½ teaspoon **dried pink peppercorns**, crushed

⅔ cup **red wine**

2½ cups **Chicken Stock** (see page 17)

salt and **pepper**

CROUTONS:

8 slices of **French bread**

4 thin slices from a **goat cheese** log, cut in half

10

PREP

55

COOK

4

SERVES

posh

Red onion soup with goat cheese

Make sure you choose a soft goat cheese for the croutons. The cheese needs to soften and begin to melt and bubble; hard varieties won't do this successfully. Also, pick a fairly decent red wine—using cheap wine for cooking is a false economy.

1 Heat the oil in a large, heavy saucepan, add the onions, fennel, and garlic and cook over a moderate heat for 5 minutes or until softened. Sprinkle with a little salt, then reduce the heat, cover, and cook for 30–35 minutes. Increase the heat, add the vinegar and boil for 1–2 minutes until the liquid is reduced by half.

2 Add the bay leaf, thyme, peppercorns, wine, and stock. Bring to a boil, then reduce the heat and simmer for 10–15 minutes. Remove the thyme and bay leaf and taste and adjust the seasoning if necessary.

3 Meanwhile, make the croutons. Put the bread slices under a preheated hot broiler and toast lightly on one side. Turn the slices over and top each one with a slice of goat cheese. Return to the broiler and toast until the cheese is bubbling and browned. Serve immediately with the hot soup in warm bowls.

Zucchini and mint soup

Zucchini, mint, and lemon make a delicately flavored soup, which is thickened with egg yolks and finished with a generous helping of heavy cream.

1 Melt the butter in a large, heavy saucepan, add the onion and garlic and cook over a moderate heat for 5 minutes or until softened. Stir in the zucchini and lemon zest and cook for 5–10 minutes until tender. Add the stock or water and mint and bring to a boil, then reduce the heat and simmer for 5 minutes.

2 In a blender or food processor, blend the soup in batches until smooth. Strain through a sieve into the pan. The soup can be prepared ahead up to this point.

3 Just before serving, reheat the soup to just below boiling point. In a small bowl, mix the egg yolks and cream and beat in a ladleful of the hot soup. Beat the mixture into the soup and heat gently without boiling. Season to taste with salt and pepper and serve immediately in warm soup bowls.

20

PREP

25

COOK

4

SERVES

herby

¼ cup **butter**

1 small **onion**, chopped

1–2 **garlic cloves**, crushed

1½ lb **zucchini**, diced

finely grated zest of 1 **lemon**

2½ cups **Chicken Stock** (see page 17) or **water**

2–3 tablespoons chopped **mint**

2 **egg yolks**

½ cup **heavy cream**

salt and **pepper**

3 teaspoons **cumin seeds**

3 tablespoons **olive oil**

1 **onion**, chopped

1 **garlic clove**, crushed

4 **red bell peppers**, roasted, skinned, seeded (see page 90), and diced

4 cups **Chicken Stock** (see page 17)

salt and **pepper**

CILANTRO OIL:

¾ cup fresh **cilantro**, including stalks

½ cup extra virgin **olive oil**

45

PREP

55

COOK

4

SERVES

spicy

Roasted red pepper and cumin soup

Roasted peppers have a sweet, smoky flavor and they need few other ingredients. Here, they are combined with just a few herbs and spices, as well as fresh chicken stock. Use the cilantro oil within 1 week of making.

1 Make the cilantro oil. Blanch the cilantro for 5–10 seconds in a saucepan of boiling water. Drain and refresh in cold water. Drain well and squeeze out all the liquid in a clean dish towel. Chop roughly. In a blender or food processor, blend the cilantro with the oil until very smooth. Strain through a fine sieve, then through 2 layers of cheesecloth or a paper coffee filter, put in a clean bottle and refrigerate.

2 Put the cumin seeds in a dry, nonstick skillet and cook over a low heat for 2–3 minutes. Allow to cool, then grind finely in a spice grinder or in a mortar with a pestle.

3 Heat the oil in a large saucepan, add the onion and garlic and cook over a moderate heat for 5 minutes or until softened. Add the peppers, cumin, and stock. Bring to a boil. Reduce the heat and simmer for 10 minutes.

4 In a blender or food processor, blend the soup in batches until smooth. Strain through a fine sieve into the pan. Reheat gently. Season to taste with salt and pepper. Serve in warm soup bowls drizzled with the cilantro oil.

Red pepper and potato soup

This easy-to-make soup is ideal for a midweek supper. Don't add too much seasoning or you will overpower the flavor of the red peppers. If you are using dried rosemary, you need half the amount of the fresh herb.

1 Heat the oil in a large, heavy saucepan, add the garlic, onion and bell peppers and cook over a moderate heat for 5 minutes or until softened.

2 Add the stock, rosemary, sugar, and tomato paste. Stir well, then add the potatoes. Bring to a boil. Reduce the heat, partially cover, and simmer for 40–45 minutes or until the vegetables are very tender.

3 In the blender or food processor, blend the soup in batches until smooth, then transfer it to a clean saucepan. Season to taste with salt and pepper. Reheat gently and serve in warm soup bowls.

15
PREP

50
COOK

4
SERVES

easy

3 tablespoons **olive oil**

1 **garlic clove**, chopped

1 **onion**, chopped

2 **red bell peppers**, cored, seeded, and chopped

5 cups **Vegetable Stock** (see page 19)

½ teaspoon finely chopped **rosemary**

¼ teaspoon **superfine sugar**

2 tablespoons **tomato paste**

2 cups chopped **potatoes**

salt and **pepper**

2–3 large **eggplants**, about 2 lb in total

3 tablespoons **olive oil**

1 **red onion**

2 **garlic cloves**, crushed

5 cups **Chicken Stock** (see page 17)

¾ cup **crème fraîche** or **Greek** or **whole milk yogurt**

2 tablespoons chopped **mint**

salt and **pepper**

15

PREP

40

COOK

4

SERVES

tasty

Roasted eggplant soup

Eggplants contain a lot of liquid, and broiling or roasting is one way of drying them out before cooking, although they will still need to be pressed to extract more liquid before you use them.

1 Put the eggplants under a preheated hot broiler and cook, turning occasionally, for 20 minutes or until the skin is well charred and the flesh has softened. Allow to cool slightly. Cut the eggplants in half, scoop out the flesh, and chop.

2 Heat the oil in a large, heavy-based saucepan, add the onion and garlic and cook over a moderate heat for 5 minutes or until softened. Add the chopped eggplant and the stock and cook for 10–15 minutes.

3 In a blender or food processor, blend the soup in batches until smooth. Strain through a sieve into the pan. Reheat gently and season to taste with salt and pepper.

4 Mix the yogurt with the mint and season to taste with salt and pepper. Serve the soup in warm soup bowls, garnished with a spoonful of the minted crème fraîche or yogurt.

Cream of celeriac soup

Celeriac is a knobbly root vegetable that is a type of celery. Its distinctive flavor makes a delicious soup. Choose firm, small roots—large roots may be hollow or woody inside.

10 PREP

30 COOK

4 SERVES

rich

¼ cup **butter**

2 **shallots** or 1 **onion**, chopped

1 **garlic clove**, crushed

1 lb **celeriac**, diced

4 cups **Chicken Stock** (see page 17)

1¼ cups **light cream** or **milk**

½ cup whole blanched **almonds**

salt and **pepper**

1 Melt the butter in a large, heavy saucepan, add the shallots or onion and garlic and cook over a moderate heat for 5 minutes or until softened. Add the celeriac, cover, and cook for 5–10 minutes until the celeriac softens. Add the stock and bring to a boil, then reduce the heat and simmer for 10–15 minutes.

2 In a blender or food processor, blend the soup in batches until smooth, then return it to the pan. Stir in the cream or milk and season to taste with salt and pepper. Reheat gently without boiling.

3 Meanwhile, heat a dry, nonstick skillet over a moderate heat. Add the almonds and cook, turning frequently, for 5 minutes or until lightly browned and toasted. Tip out of the pan and allow to cool slightly. Grind in a spice grinder or in a mortar with a pestle.

4 Serve the hot soup in warm soup bowls, sprinkled with the ground toasted almonds.

¼ cup **butter**

1 **onion**, finely chopped

8 oz **potatoes**, cut into
½ inch cubes

10 oz prepared
watercress

4 cups **Vegetable Stock**
(see page 19)

1¼ cups **light cream**

12 **quails' eggs**

⅔ cup finely grated
Parmesan cheese,
to serve

salt and **pepper**

10

PREP

25

COOK

4

SERVES

party

Watercress soup with quails' eggs

This is a great soup for a special occasion, but it is quick and easy to prepare, so makes an ideal dish for a dinner party. Quails' eggs are a lovely garnish, as well as adding substance to the soup.

1 Melt the butter in a large, heavy saucepan, add the onion and cook over a low heat for 8–10 minutes or until softened. Stir in the potatoes and watercress, cover, and cook, stirring once or twice, for 3–5 minutes until the watercress has just wilted.

2 Add the stock and season to taste with salt and pepper. Bring to a boil and cook for 6–8 minutes or until the potatoes are tender.

3 In a blender or food processor, blend the soup in batches until smooth. Strain through a sieve into the pan. Add the cream and taste and adjust the seasoning if necessary. Reheat gently without boiling.

4 Meanwhile, poach the eggs in a saucepan of gently simmering water, drain well and put 3 eggs in each bowl. Ladle the soup over the quail eggs and serve sprinkled with grated Parmesan.

Garlic soup with Parmesan dumplings

This hearty soup has an Italian feel, with plenty of garlic and fresh herbs. The dumplings can be prepared in advance, and they will soak up the flavors of the soup as they cook in the liquid.

30* PREP

55 COOK

4 SERVES

stylish

1 Make the Parmesan dumplings. Put all the ingredients in a bowl and mix to form a firm paste. Season to taste with salt and pepper and nutmeg. Cover and chill for 1 hour. With lightly floured hands, form into 24 small balls, roll in flour, and put on a tray.

2 Make the soup. Heat the oil in a large, heavy saucepan, add the garlic cloves and onions and cook over a moderate heat for 5 minutes. Reduce the heat, cover tightly, and cook for 30–35 minutes until tender. Do not allow to brown.

3 Add the potatoes, bay leaf, thyme, saffron, stock, and milk. Season to taste with salt and pepper. Bring to a boil, then reduce the heat and simmer for 20–30 minutes. Add the spinach and cook for 1–2 minutes until wilted.

4 In a blender or food processor, blend the soup in batches until smooth. Strain through a sieve into a clean saucepan. Return to a boil and add the dumplings. Simmer for 3–4 minutes until the dumplings are light and cooked through. Serve immediately.

* Plus 1 hour chilling

5 tablespoons **olive oil**

2 small heads of **garlic**, cloves separated and peeled

2 **onions**, sliced

1 lb **potatoes**, diced

1 **bay leaf**

1 sprig of **thyme**

pinch of **saffron threads**

5 cups **Chicken Stock** (see page 17)

2½ cups **milk**

2 cups finely shredded **spinach**

salt and **pepper**

PARMESAN DUMPLINGS:

¾ cup **ricotta cheese**

2 tablespoons **butter**, softened

⅓ cup finely grated **Parmesan cheese**

1 teaspoon finely grated **lemon zest**

2 tablespoons **all-purpose flour**

2 **egg yolks**, beaten

grated nutmeg

2 tablespoons **vegetable oil**

1 **onion**, finely chopped

1–2 **garlic cloves**, crushed

1 **red chili**, seeded, and finely chopped

1 inch piece of fresh **gingerroot**, peeled and grated

finely grated zest and juice of 1 **lime**

2 large **tomatoes**, skinned and chopped, about 10 oz

2 large semi-ripe **plantains**

6 **allspice berries**, crushed

1 sprig of **thyme**

5 cups **Chicken Stock** (see page 17)

1¾ cups canned **coconut milk**

¾ cup skinned **Brazil nuts**

salt and **pepper**

20

PREP

60

COOK

6

SERVES

tasty

Coconut and plantain soup

This delicious recipe combines creamy coconut milk with hot red chili and plantain to produce a soup with a distinctive Creole flavor. The Brazil nuts add an unusual crunchy finish.

1 Heat the oil in a large, heavy saucepan, add the onion, garlic, chili, ginger, and lime zest and cook over a low heat for 8–10 minutes or until softened. Add the tomatoes and cook for 5 minutes.

2 Use a small, sharp knife to cut off one end of the plantains. Slit the skins lengthwise and unpeel sideways. Chop the flesh. Add to the pan with the allspice, thyme, stock, and coconut milk. Season to taste with salt and pepper and bring to a boil. Reduce the heat and simmer for 30 minutes.

3 Meanwhile, spread the Brazil nuts on a baking sheet, then roast in a preheated oven, 325°F, for about 10–15 minutes until lightly golden. Remove from the oven and allow to cool, then chop finely.

4 Remove and discard the thyme from the soup. In a blender or food processor, blend the soup in batches until smooth. Strain through a sieve into the pan. Reheat gently. Add the lime juice. Serve in warm bowls sprinkled with the chopped Brazil nuts.

Chestnut and bacon soup

40

PREP

55

COOK

You don't need a lot of pancetta to add flavor to a soup. Shallots are much sweeter than regular onions, so opt for these if you can. If you cannot find fresh chestnuts, use 8 oz vacuum-packed, cooked chestnuts instead.

4

SERVES

feast

12 oz **chestnuts**

¼ cup **butter**

3 oz rindless **pancetta** or **bacon**, chopped

3 **shallots** or 1 large **onion**, chopped

½ small **fennel bulb**, trimmed and chopped

1 **celery stick**, chopped

2½ cups **Chicken Stock** (see page 17)

2½ cups **milk**

salt and **pepper**

1 Cut a slash in the pointed end of each chestnut. Place in a saucepan, cover with cold water and bring to a boil, then reduce the heat and simmer for 2 minutes. Remove from the heat. Using a slotted spoon, lift out one chestnut at a time and remove and discard the outer and inner skins. If the skins are hard to peel, return the pan to a boil and repeat.

2 Melt the butter in a large, heavysaucepan, add the pancetta or bacon and cook over a moderate heat, stirring, for 2–3 minutes or until lightly browned. Reduce the heat and add the shallots or onion, fennel, and celery. Cook for 6–8 minutes until softened.

3 Add the chestnuts, stock, and the milk. Season with salt and pepper. Bring to a boil, then reduce the heat and simmer for 30–40 minutes or until the chestnuts are tender.

4 In the blender or food processor, blend the soup in batches until smooth. Strain through a sieve into the pan. Return to a boil. Serve immediately in warm soup bowls.

3 tablespoons **olive oil**

1 **onion**, chopped

2½ cups **peas**, thawed if frozen

5 cups **Chicken Stock** (see page 17)

1 cup **arborio rice**

pinch of **superfine sugar**

2 tablespoons chopped **flat leaf parsley**

⅔ cup finely grated **Parmesan cheese**, plus extra to serve

salt and **pepper**

TO GARNISH:

4 slices of **prosciutto**

1 tablespoon **olive oil**

10

PREP

30

COOK

4

SERVES

party

Risi e bisi with frazzled prosciutto

Although it's nice to use fresh peas and pod them yourself, frozen peas are actually just as nutritious. Peas are generally frozen very soon after being picked, so the vitamins are fully preserved.

1 Heat the oil in a large, heavy saucepan, add the onion and cook over a moderate heat for 5 minutes or until softened.

2 Add the stock and bring to a boil, then reduce the heat and stir in the rice. If you are using fresh peas, add them now and simmer gently for 5 minutes before adding the rice. Season to taste with salt and pepper and add the sugar. Cover and simmer gently, stirring occasionally, for 15–20 minutes until the rice is tender. If you are using frozen peas, add them after 10–15 minutes.

3 Meanwhile, cut each prosciutto slice in half lengthwise. Heat the oil in a large, nonstick skillet, add the prosciutto strips and cook over a high heat for 10–15 seconds or until crisp. Drain on paper towels.

4 Stir the parsley and Parmesan into the hot soup, ladle into warm soup bowls, and top with 2 pieces of the frazzled prosciutto. Serve with a small bowl of extra Parmesan to hand round separately.

Bread soup

The title may not sound very appealing, but this is an absolutely delicious and warming soup. It couldn't be easier to make, but will impress your friends.

1 Warm a large tureen or casserole by filling it with boiling water and allowing it to stand for a few minutes.

2 In a blender or food processor, blend the cilantro, garlic, and salt with 2–4 tablespoons of the oil to make a smooth paste.

3 Discard the water from the tureen or casserole and put the cilantro paste in the bottom. Drizzle over the remaining oil, then pour over the measured boiling water and stir in the bread cubes. They will absorb the liquid and become soggy.

4 Poach the eggs in a pan of simmering water. Serve the soup in warm soup bowls, with a poached egg in each, sprinkled with the parsley.

10

PREP

5

COOK

4

SERVES

stylish

¼ cup fresh **cilantro**

4 **garlic cloves**, roughly chopped

1 tablespoon coarse **sea salt**

8 tablespoons extra virgin **olive oil**

6 cups boiling **water**

12 oz day-old **ciabatta** or **pugliese**, crusts removed, broken or cut into 1 inch cubes

4 **eggs**

2 tablespoons chopped **flat leaf parsley**

pinch of **saffron threads**

½ cup boiling **water**

1½ lb **mussels**, scrubbed and debearded

¾ cup **dry white wine**

2 tablespoons **olive oil**

2 **shallots**, finely chopped

1 **garlic clove**, finely chopped

¾ cup **heavy cream**

4½ cups **baby spinach**

15 **basil** leaves, shredded

30

PREP

20

COOK

4

SERVES

herby

Mussel soup with basil and spinach

Mussels take well to many different flavors and soak up the juices they are cooked in. Shallots, garlic, and wine are ideal accompaniments, and they are combined here with saffron and spinach.

1 Put the saffron in a small heatproof bowl and pour over the measured boiling water. Allow to soak. Discard any mussels that are broken or open, or that do not close when tapped on a work surface. Put them in a large colander over a bowl.

2 Pour the wine into a large, heavy saucepan. Bring to a boil. Add the mussels, cover tightly, and cook, shaking the pan frequently, for 2–3 minutes or until all the mussels have opened.

3 Tip the mussels into the colander and remove from their shells, discarding any that have not opened. Strain the liquid through a cheesecloth-lined sieve and set aside.

4 Heat the oil in a saucepan, add the shallots and garlic and cook over a low heat for 5–6 minutes. Add the strained mussel liquid, cream, and saffron and its infused liquid and bring to a boil, reduce the heat and add the spinach, half of the basil, and all the mussels. Simmer for 2 minutes, then remove from the heat, stir in the remaining basil, and serve.

Crab, asparagus, and lemon soup

20
PREP

60
COOK

4
SERVES

posh

This luxurious soup requires a freshly cooked crab in the shell. Ask the fish merchant to remove all the white and brown meat for you, but remember to ask for the shell, in order to make the stock. To break the shell into small pieces, put it into a plastic bag and smash with a rolling pin.

1 Put the crab shell in a large, heavy saucepan. Cover with 5 cups of the measured water. Bring to a boil. Reduce the heat and simmer for 30 minutes. Strain through a fine sieve into a clean saucepan.

2 Bring the remaining water to a boil in a separate saucepan with a pinch of salt. Add the asparagus and simmer for 2–3 minutes until just tender. Drain, reserving the liquid, refresh in cold water and drain again.

3 Return the crab stock to a boil. Add the asparagus water and the rice and simmer gently for 12–15 minutes until tender.

4 In a bowl, mix together the cream cheese, 5 tablespoons of the brown crab meat, and salt and pepper and cayenne pepper to taste. Spread each toast slice with the mixture.

5 In a small bowl, mix together the egg yolks and lemon juice. Beat in a ladleful of the stock. Beat the egg mixture into the pan. Do not boil. Add the asparagus and white crab meat and heat through. Serve sprinkled with chervil and accompanied by the toasts.

1 freshly cooked **crab**, about 1½ lb, white and brown meat removed and shell broken into small pieces

7 cups **water**

8 oz fine young **asparagus**, cut into 2 inch pieces

⅓ cup **white long-grain rice**

3 tablespoons **cream cheese**

cayenne pepper

8 thin slices of French **bread**, toasted

3 **egg yolks**

2 tablespoons **lemon juice**

salt and **pepper**

sprigs of **chervil**, to garnish

asian

1¼ cups **Chicken Stock** (see page 17)

3 **kaffir lime leaves**, torn in half

½ **lemon grass stalk**, obliquely sliced

1 inch piece of **galangal**, peeled and thinly sliced

½ cup **coconut milk**

4 tablespoons **Thai fish sauce**

1 teaspoon **palm sugar** or **light brown sugar**

3 tablespoons **lime juice**

4 oz **chicken**, skinned and cut into bite-size pieces

2 tablespoons **chili oil** or 2 **small chilies**, thinly sliced (optional)

PREP

COOK

4

SERVES

easy

Chicken and coconut milk soup

This quantity of soup is enough for 1 large bowl of soup shared between 4 people or 4 small, individual bowls. If you would like to serve the soup as a first course on its own, in Western style, just double the quantities.

1 Pour the stock into a large, heavy saucepan and bring to a boil. Stir in the lime leaves, lemon grass, and galangal. Reduce the heat to a simmer. Add the coconut milk, fish sauce, sugar, and lime juice and stir well, then add the chicken pieces and simmer for 5 minutes.

2 Just before serving, add the chili oil or chilies (if using) and stir again. Serve the soup immediately in warm soup bowls.

Noodle soup with chicken

This soup is sufficient on its own for a light meal for 4 people. If you wish to serve it as part of a Thai meal, you should halve or even quarter the quantities.

1 Put the stock, star anise, cinnamon stick pieces, pickled garlic, vinegar, fish sauce, cilantro, sugar, and soy sauce in a large, heavy saucepan and bring slowly to a boil. Add the chicken pieces and simmer for 4 minutes. Add the bok choy and bean sprouts and simmer for an additional 2 minutes.

2 Meanwhile, make the crispy shallots. Heat the oil in a wok or deep skillet. Finely chop the shallots. Add to the hot oil and cook, stirring, for 40 seconds or until sizzling and golden. Remove with a slotted spoon and spread out on paper towels to drain.

3 Divide the rice sticks between 4 large soup bowls and ladle over the soup. Sprinkle the cilantro leaves on top and garnish with the crispy shallots.

15

PREP

15

COOK

4

SERVES

classic

5 cups **Chicken Stock** (see page 17)

1 **star anise**

3 inch piece of **cinnamon stick**, broken

2 bulbs **pickled garlic**, finely chopped

4 tablespoons **pickled garlic vinegar**

½ cup **Thai fish sauce**

8 fresh **cilantro roots**, finely chopped

4 teaspoons **palm sugar**

4 teaspoons **soy sauce**

7 oz **chicken**, skinned and diced

2 cups roughly chopped **bok choy**

½ cup **bean sprouts**

7 oz **rice sticks**, cooked

3 tablespoons fresh **cilantro**

CRISPY SHALLOTS:

about 3 cups **peanut oil**

2 **shallots**

7 fl oz canned **coconut milk**, shaken

¾ cup **Chicken Stock** (see page 17)

2 **lemon grass stalks** (white part only), each 5 inches long and bruised

2 inches fresh **galangal**, peeled and cut into several pieces

15 **black peppercorns**, crushed

13 oz boneless, skinless **chicken breast**

1 tablespoon **Thai fish sauce**

1 tablespoon **palm sugar**

5 oz **mixed mushrooms**, such as oyster, shiitake or button

8 oz **cherry tomatoes**

2–3 tablespoons **lime juice** or **lemon juice**

5 **kaffir lime leaves**, torn in half

3–5 small **red and green chilies**, bruised

fresh **cilantro**, to garnish

15

PREP

15

COOK

4

SERVES

fresh

Chicken, coconut, and galangal soup

Here is a classic Thai dish that is enjoyed by adults and children alike. The galangal and lemon grass give it plenty of flavor, but it is not too hot.

1 Put the coconut milk, stock, lemon grass, galangal, and peppercorns in a large, heavy saucepan or wok and slowly bring to a boil.

2 Slice the chicken, then add to the pan with the fish sauce and sugar. Reduce the heat and simmer, stirring constantly, for 5 minutes or until the chicken is cooked through.

3 Halve the mushrooms if they are large and remove and discard the hard stalks. Add to the pan with the tomatoes and simmer for 2–3 minutes, taking care that the tomatoes do not lose their shape. Add the lime or lemon juice, lime leaves, and chilies for the last few seconds of cooking.

4 Serve the soup immediately in warm soup bowls, garnished with a few cilantro leaves.

Thai chicken and coconut soup

Thai red curry paste adds the essential fiery heat to this soup, while the kaffir lime leaves add a sharp citrus punch. Fresh kaffir lime leaves can be found in specialist Asian stores and gourmet markets. The leaves can be stored in the refrigerator for up to a month or in the freezer for months at a time.

1 Heat the oil in a wok or deep, nonstick skillet, add the curry paste and stir-fry for 1 minute until sizzling. Add the chicken and lime leaves and stir-fry for 1 minute until evenly coated in the curry paste.

2 Add the stock and bring to a boil. Reduce the heat, cover, and simmer for 15 minutes. Add all of the remaining ingredients to the pan and simmer gently for an additional 2–3 minutes.

3 Spoon the soup into warm soup bowls and serve topped with basil leaves, sliced red chili and shredded lime leaves.

15

PREP

20

COOK

4

SERVES

hot

2 tablespoons **vegetable oil**

1–2 tablespoons **Thai red curry paste**

1½ lb boneless, skinless **chicken breast**, diced

8 **kaffir lime leaves**

2½ cups **Chicken Stock** (see page 17)

8 oz **green beans**, trimmed and halved

1 **red bell pepper**, cored, seeded, and sliced

1⅔ cups canned **coconut milk**

1 tablespoon **Thai fish sauce**

TO GARNISH:

Thai basil or ordinary **basil** leaves

sliced **red chili**

shredded **kaffir lime leaves**

2½ cups **Chicken Stock** (see page 17)

2 **garlic cloves**, sliced

4 oz **ground pork**

3 dried **black fungus**, soaked in hot water for 20 minutes, drained and sliced

2 tablespoons **light soy sauce**

1 tablespoon **Thai fish sauce**

2 oz dried **rice vermicelli**, soaked in hot water for 15–20 minutes and cut into 2 inch lengths

10*

PREP

10

COOK

4

SERVES

simple

Pork ball and black fungus soup

This soup is so simple and quick to prepare. Soak the black fungus and vermicelli in advance so that everything is ready to go when you want to eat.

1 Heat the stock in a wok or large, heavy saucepan and add the garlic.

2 Shape the pork into small round balls. Drop them into the simmering stock and cook for 5 minutes.

3 Add the black fungus, soy sauce, fish sauce, and rice vermicelli and simmer for about 2 minutes. Serve immediately in warm soup bowls.

* Plus 20 minutes soaking

Pork and bamboo shoot soup

This recipe uses plenty of garlic, so it might not be the best choice for a romantic dinner! However, it should keep those colds at bay, and the soup isn't dominated by garlic; it blends well with the pork.

10
PREP

12
COOK

4
SERVES

tasty

1 Heat the stock in a wok or large, heavy saucepan and then add the peppercorns and crushed and chopped garlic.

2 Meanwhile, mix the pork with the soy sauce and pepper, then shape into small balls. Drop the balls into the simmering stock and cook for 4 minutes.

3 Add the bamboo shoots and simmer gently for 5 minutes. Add the fish sauce and stir well. Serve in warm soup bowls, garnished with the scallion and cilantro leaves.

2 cups **Chicken Stock** (see page 17)

10 **black peppercorns**, crushed

7 **garlic cloves**, 2 crushed, 5 roughly chopped

4 oz **ground pork**

1½ tablespoons **light soy sauce**

pinch of **pepper**

¾ cup **bamboo shoots**

3 tablespoons **Thai fish sauce**

TO GARNISH:

1 **scallion**, obliquely sliced

fresh **cilantro**

6 oz fresh **egg noodles**

1 teaspoon **garlic oil**

2 **choi sum**, sliced

1 tablespoon thinly sliced **scallions**

1 tablespoon **light soy sauce**

1 tablespoon fresh **cilantro**

pinch of **pepper**

8 oz **roast pork**, sliced

2½ cups **Chicken Stock** (see page 17)

DIPPING SAUCE:

4 tablespoons distilled **white vinegar**

2–3 tablespoons **Thai fish sauce**

1 large **red chili**, sliced

15

PREP

10

COOK

4

SERVES

stylish

Pork and noodle soup

Choi sum is a type of Chinese green leafy vegetable. If you cannot find it, you can use other Chinese greens, such as bok choy, instead. For a really authentic dish, use pork that has first been marinaded in a red pork sauce, available from Asian markets.

1 Bring a large saucepan of water to a boil, add the egg noodles and boil for 2–3 minutes, untangling while boiling. Drain well and return to the pan. Add the garlic oil and toss to coat, to prevent sticking together.

2 Meanwhile, make the dipping sauce. Combine all the ingredients in a small bowl.

3 Blanch the choi sum in a separate saucepan of boiling water for 1 minute, then drain.

4 Put the cooked noodles in a large, heat-proof serving bowl. Add the choi sum, scallions, soy sauce, cilantro, and pepper. Arrange the pork slices on the top.

5 Heat the stock in a saucepan to boiling point, then pour over the pork, noodles, and vegetables. Serve the soup immediately with the dipping sauce.

Pork ball and tofu soup

Tofu is believed to have many health benefits, and it is a staple ingredient in many Asian cuisines. It's very versatile and, although fairly bland on its own, can absorb other flavors easily.

1 Heat the stock with the chopped and halved garlic, pepper, and cilantro in a large, heavy saucepan.

2 Meanwhile, make the pork balls. Mix the pork with the soy sauce and pepper, then shape into small balls. Drop the balls into the simmering stock and cook for 4 minutes.

3 Add the tofu, laver, and soy sauce, stir for 30 seconds, then serve the soup in warm soup bowls, garnished with cilantro leaves.

15

PREP

10

COOK

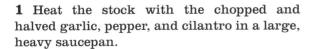

4

SERVES

quick

2½ cups **Chicken Stock** (see page 17)

5 **garlic cloves**, 1 finely chopped, 4 halved

½ teaspoon **pepper**

8 fresh **cilantro roots**, roughly chopped

1 cup **silken tofu**, cut into 1 inch slices

1 sheet roasted **laver**, torn into shreds

2 tablespoons **light soy sauce**

fresh **cilantro**, to garnish

PORK BALLS:

2½ oz **ground pork**

1 tablespoon **light soy sauce**

½ teaspoon **pepper**

4 dried, long **red chilies**, about 5 inches long, or 4 dried, small **red chilies**, about 2 inches long

7 **shallots**, roughly chopped

4 **garlic cloves**, roughly chopped

1 teaspoon **shrimp paste**

5 cups **Vegetable Stock** (see page 19)

12 oz **ground pork**

12 oz **snake beans**, cut into 1 inch pieces

2 tablespoons **Thai fish sauce**

5 tablespoons **lemon juice**

15

PREP

8

COOK

6

SERVES

exotic

Sour pork soup with snake beans

In Thailand, this slightly hot and sour soup is a popular addition to a main meal. Snake beans are narrow, round, and stringless beans, 12–36 inches long, and can be found in Thai or Asian markets. Green beans can be used if you have trouble finding them.

1 Cut off the stalks of the chilies, then slit the chilies lengthwise with a sharp knife. Remove and discard all the seeds and chop the flesh roughly. Put it in a heatproof bowl, cover with hot water, and allow to soak for 2 minutes or until softened, then drain.

2 Put the chilies, shallots, garlic, and shrimp paste in a mortar and pound with a pestle to form a smooth paste.

3 Pour the stock into a large, heavy saucepan and bring to a boil. Stir in the chili paste, then reduce the heat to moderate.

4 Shape the pork into small balls. Drop the balls into the simmering stock with the beans, fish sauce, and lemon juice. Cook for 4–5 minutes. Spoon the soup into a serving bowl and serve immediately.

Rice soup with ground pork

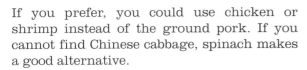

If you prefer, you could use chicken or shrimp instead of the ground pork. If you cannot find Chinese cabbage, spinach makes a good alternative.

15

PREP

10

COOK

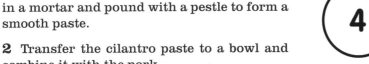

1 Put the cilantro roots, garlic, and pepper in a mortar and pound with a pestle to form a smooth paste.

2 Transfer the cilantro paste to a bowl and combine it with the pork.

3 Put the stock in a large, heavy saucepan and bring to a boil. Add the soy sauce, preserved radish (if using), and rice.

4 Shape the pork mixture into small balls. Drop the balls into the simmering soup and cook for 3 minutes.

5 Add the ginger and Chinese cabbage. Cook for an additional 1–2 minutes. Spoon the soup into a serving bowl. Garnish with the scallions and cilantro leaves. Season to taste with pepper and serve immediately.

4

SERVES

filling

3 fresh **cilantro roots**, roughly chopped

3 **garlic cloves**, roughly chopped

¼ teaspoon **white pepper**

13 oz **ground pork**

7½ cups **Vegetable Stock** (see page 19)

3 tablespoons **light soy sauce**

1 tablespoon **preserved radish**, finely chopped (optional)

4 cups **jasmine rice**

1 inch piece of fresh **gingerroot**, peeled and thinly sliced

¾ cup roughly chopped **Chinese cabbage leaves**

TO SERVE:

2 **scallions**, finely chopped

fresh **cilantro**

white pepper

6 cups **Chicken Stock** (see page 17)

2 **lemon grass stalks**, bruised

small piece of fresh **gingerroot**, peeled and thinly sliced

2 tablespoons **light soy sauce**

2 tablespoons **lime juice**

2 teaspoons **dark brown sugar**

4 oz dried flat **rice noodles**

9 oz **sirloin steak**, sliced

TO SERVE:

1½ cups **bean sprouts**

1 **red chili**, thinly sliced

handful of **Thai basil**

handful of **mint**

15

PREP

20

COOK

4

SERVES

classic

Vietnamese beef pho

This is the national dish of Vietnam: a spicy, fragrant broth served with rice noodles, bean sprouts, aromatic herbs, and slices of rare beef. Save this comforting dish for a night when it's cold and raining outside, and you feel in need of a spiritual and physical uplift.

1 Put the stock, lemon grass, ginger, soy sauce, lime juice, and sugar in a large, heavy saucepan and bring to a boil. Reduce the heat and simmer gently for 10 minutes.

2 Using a slotted spoon, remove the lemon grass and ginger and discard. Add the rice noodles and cook according to the package instructions, adding the sliced steak for the last 2–3 minutes.

3 Spoon the pho into warm soup bowls, top with the bean sprouts, chili, basil, and mint and serve immediately.

Hot and sour shrimp soup

Hot and sour is a common combination in Chinese food, much like sweet and sour. Here, the heat comes from the chili oil, while lime juice offers the "sour" element of the recipe.

10

PREP

20

COOK

4

SERVES

hot

1 Put the stock, lime leaves, lemon grass, galangal, sugar, lime juice, and chili oil or chopped chilies in a large wok or heavy saucepan and bring to a boil. Reduce the heat and simmer gently for 15 minutes.

2 Add the shrimp just before serving; they will turn pink in a few seconds and will be cooked through after 1 minute.

3 Season to taste with salt and pepper and serve the soup in one large bowl or individual bowls, garnished with cilantro sprigs.

5 cups **Fish Stock** (see page 16)

4 **kaffir lime leaves**, torn in half

1 **lemon grass stalk**, thinly and obliquely sliced

1 inch piece of **galangal**, peeled and sliced

1 tablespoon **palm sugar** or **light brown sugar**

5 tablespoons **lime juice**

2 tablespoons **chili oil** or 12 small **green chilies**, chopped

12–16 raw peeled **shrimp**

salt and **pepper**

sprigs of fresh **cilantro**, to garnish

4 oz dried **soba noodles**

2 teaspoons **sesame oil**

1 bunch of **scallions**, sliced

2 **bok choy**, shredded

7½ cups hot **Vegetable Stock** (see page 19)

4 tablespoons **sake**

2 tablespoons **dark soy sauce**

1 cup **bean sprouts**

vegetable oil, for deep-frying

12 raw **jumbo shrimp**, peeled and deveined

2 sheets of **nori**, shredded

TEMPURA:

1 **egg yolk**

½ cup **all-purpose flour**

¼ cup iced **water**

20

PREP

10

COOK

4

SERVES

stylish

Noodle soup with shrimp tempura

Nori is a type of dried seaweed that you will usually find wrapped around sushi. It is now widely available in supermarkets and is used here as a garnish.

1 Cook the soba noodles according to the package instructions. Drain well.

2 Heat the sesame oil in a large wok, add the scallions and bok choy and stir-fry for 1 minute. Add the stock, sake, and soy sauce and simmer gently for 5 minutes. Stir in the bean sprouts.

3 Meanwhile, make the tempura. In a bowl, briefly beat together the egg yolk, flour, and water to make a slightly lumpy batter. Heat the vegetable oil in a separate wok, a deep, heavy saucepan, or a deep-fat fryer to 350–375°F, or until a cube of bread browns in 30 seconds. Dip the shrimp in the batter, then drop them into the hot oil and cook for 3 minutes or until golden. Remove with a slotted spoon and drain on paper towels.

4 Spoon the noodles into warm soup bowls, add the soup and top with the shrimp and strips of nori. Serve immediately.

Hot and sour soup with seafood

This is one of the most popular soups in Thai cuisine. If you prefer, you can include chicken, beef, or lamb instead of the seafood.

1 Put the stock, lemon grass, cilantro and fish sauce in a saucepan and bring to a boil.

2 Reduce the heat, add the seafood and simmer for 2 minutes.

3 Cut any large mushrooms into quarters and add the mushrooms, onion, chilies, tomatoes, torn lime leaves, and lime or lemon juice to the pan. Cook for 2–3 minutes, taking care not to let the tomatoes lose their shape.

4 Turn the soup into a serving bowl, garnish with a few thinly sliced lime leaves and serve.

30
PREP

8
COOK

4
SERVES

fresh

4 cups **Fish Stock** (see page 16)

3 **lemon grass stalks** (white part only), each 5 inches long, bruised

5 fresh **cilantro roots**, bruised

2 tablespoons **Thai fish sauce**

1¼ lb prepared mixed seafood, such as raw **shrimp**, **squid**, **white fish** fillet (cod or sea bass), **scallops**, and **mussels**, cut into bite-size pieces

4 oz **straw mushrooms**

1 **onion**, quartered

4–5 small **red and green chilies**, slightly crushed

12 **cherry tomatoes**

5 **kaffir lime leaves**, torn in half, plus extra, thinly sliced, to garnish

3 tablespoons **lime juice** or **lemon juice**

2 oz **mixed mushrooms**, such as oyster, chestnut, and shiitake

7½ cups **Vegetable Stock** (see page 19)

4 tablespoons **light soy sauce**

1 tablespoon **preserved radish**, finely chopped (optional)

4 cups boiled **jasmine rice**

10 oz prepared mixed seafood, such as raw **shrimp**, **squid**, **white fish** fillet (cod or sea bass,) and **scallops**, cut into bite-size pieces

1 inch piece of fresh **gingerroot**, peeled and thinly sliced

white pepper

TO GARNISH:

2 **scallions**, thinly and obliquely sliced

fresh **cilantro**

30

PREP

10

COOK

4

SERVES

party

Thai rice soup with seafood

To eat in Thailand is to eat rice, and it will come as no surprise to find rice in desserts, or, as here, in soup.

1 Cut any large mushrooms in half and remove and discard the hard stalks.

2 Put the stock in a large, heavy saucepan and bring to a boil. Add the soy sauce, preserved radish (if using), and rice, reduce the heat and simmer for 2–3 minutes.

3 Add the seafood, mushrooms, and ginger and simmer for 2–3 minutes.

4 Spoon the soup into a large serving bowl, then garnish with the scallions and cilantro leaves. Season to taste with pepper and serve immediately.

Fragrant tofu and noodle soup

Lemon grass can be added whole or halved to flavor a dish, or it is sometimes finely chopped to become an ingredient. Before using it, remove the very tough outer layers of the stalks.

15* PREP

10 COOK

2 SERVES

herby

1 Put the tofu on a plate covered with paper towels. Allow to stand for 10 minutes to drain thoroughly.

2 Heat the oil in a wok or large, nonstick skillet until hot, add the tofu and stir-fry for about 2–3 minutes or until golden brown. Remove with a slotted spoon and drain on paper towels.

3 Meanwhile, soak the rice noodles in a saucepan of boiling water for 2 minutes, then drain well.

4 Put the stock in a large, heavy saucepan, add the ginger, garlic, lime leaves, and lemon grass and bring to a boil. Reduce the heat, add the tofu, noodles, spinach or bok choy, bean sprouts, and chilies and heat through for about 2 minutes. Stir in the cilantro and fish sauce, then pour into warm, deep soup bowls to serve. Serve with lime wedges and chili sauce.

¾ cup diced firm **tofu**

1 tablespoon **sesame oil**

3 oz dried fine **rice noodles**

2½ cups **Vegetable Stock** (see page 19)

1 inch piece of fresh **gingerroot**, peeled and thickly sliced

1 large **garlic clove**, thickly sliced

3 **kaffir lime leaves**, torn in half

2 **lemon grass stalks**, halved

handful of **spinach** or **bok choy** leaves

½ cup **bean sprouts**

1–2 **red chilies**, seeded, and thinly sliced

2 tablespoons fresh **cilantro**, roughly chopped

1 tablespoon **Thai fish sauce**

TO SERVE:

lime wedges

chili sauce

* Plus 10 minutes draining

2 **bitter melons**, about 10 inches long

8 oz block **ready-fried tofu**, diced

½ **onion**, chopped

1 oz dried **black fungus**, soaked in hot water for 20 minutes and drained

1 fresh **cilantro root**

2 **garlic cloves**, halved

2 tablespoons **peanut oil**

2 **eggs**

2 teaspoons **light soy sauce**

1 teaspoon **pepper**

1 teaspoon **salt**

3 cups **Vegetable Stock** (see page 19)

fresh **cilantro** leaves, to serve

CRISPY GARLIC:

about 3 cups **peanut oil**

8 cloves **garlic**, finely chopped

15*

PREP

15

COOK

4

SERVES

exotic

Stuffed bitter melon soup

This is a very unusual recipe, which uses the soup as a stock to pour over stuffed melon segments. Asian markets will stock the more specialist ingredients.

1 Make the crispy garlic. Heat the oil in a wok or deep skillet, add the garlic and cook, stirring, for 40 seconds or until sizzling and golden. Remove with a slotted spoon and spread on paper towels to drain.

2 Cut the ends off the bitter melons and discard, then cut them crosswise into 4 equal pieces. Carefully remove the seeds and pith from each piece of melon, then set aside.

3 In a blender or food processor, blend the tofu, onion, black fungus, cilantro, and garlic. Heat the oil in a wok, add the blended mixture, 1 egg, soy sauce, pepper, and salt and stir-fry for 1–2 minutes. Remove from the heat, turn into a bowl and allow to cool.

4 Add the remaining egg to the tofu mixture to bind, then use to stuff the melon pieces. Steam in a steamer for 10 minutes until cooked. Meanwhile, simmer the stock.

5 Put the melon in a serving bowl. Ladle over the hot stock. Garnish with cilantro leaves and serve sprinkled with the crispy garlic.

* Plus 20 minutes soaking

Clear soup with black fungus

This soup couldn't be simpler to make. Slice the scallions diagonally for an authentic look and serve as part of a Chinese buffet dinner.

10* PREP

7 COOK

4 SERVES

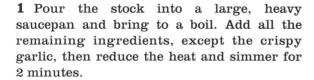

quick

1 Pour the stock into a large, heavy saucepan and bring to a boil. Add all the remaining ingredients, except the crispy garlic, then reduce the heat and simmer for 2 minutes.

2 Ladle the soup into warm soup bowls and serve hot, garnished with the crispy garlic.

2½ cups **Vegetable Stock** (see page 19)

1 teaspoon **superfine sugar**

½ teaspoon **light soy sauce**

4 oz dried **black fungus**, soaked in hot water for 20 minutes, drained, and chopped

¼ cup finely chopped **celery**, leaf and stalk

2 **scallions**, sliced lengthwise

salt and **pepper**, to taste

1 teaspoon **Crispy Garlic** (see page 208), to garnish

* Plus 20 minutes soaking

¾ cup roughly chopped **cucumber**,

1 **onion**, halved

2 **garlic cloves**, halved

¾ cup chopped **white cabbage**

2½ cups **water**

4 oz dried **bean thread noodles**, soaked, and drained

1 oz dried **tofu sheets**, soaked, drained, and torn

½ oz dried **lily flowers**, soaked and drained

1 teaspoon **salt**

1 teaspoon **superfine sugar**

½ teaspoon **light soy sauce**

2 large dried **shiitake mushrooms**, soaked, drained, and thinly sliced

chopped **celery leaves**, to garnish

PREP

10*

COOK

10

4

SERVES

stylish

Glass noodle soup

A firm favorite on restaurant menus, this is an easy dish to prepare, despite having a number of ingredients. Soak the noodles, tofu, flowers, and mushrooms in advance, according to the package instructions.

1 In a blender or food processor, blend the cucumber, onion, garlic, and cabbage for 15 seconds. Turn the mixture into a saucepan and add the measured water. Bring to a boil, then reduce the heat and simmer, stirring occasionally, for 2 minutes.

2 Strain the stock into a large, heavy saucepan and add the bean thread noodles, tofu, lily flowers, salt, sugar, and soy sauce. Stir, then cook over a moderate heat for about 3 minutes. Taste and adjust the seasoning if necessary.

3 Pour the soup into a serving bowl and arrange the mushroom slices in the center. Sprinkle with chopped celery leaves and serve immediately.

* Plus 2–3 hours soaking

Banana soup

Banana and chili make a surprisingly good pairing. Although naturally sweet, the other ingredients add the savory element, and the soup is well balanced.

1 Heat the oil in a large, heavy saucepan, add the sliced scallion and garlic and stir-fry over a high heat for 2 minutes. Add all the other ingredients, in order, then simmer for 5 minutes.

2 If liked, the soup can be blended. Set aside about one-quarter of the banana and chili slices. In a blender or food processor, blend the remaining soup in batches until smooth, then return it to the pan. Add the reserved banana and chili slices and heat through without boiling for 3 minutes.

3 Serve the soup hot, garnished with cilantro, lime quarters, and scallion strips.

15

PREP

10

COOK

4

SERVES

exotic

1 tablespoon **peanut oil**

4 **scallions**, including green shoots, sliced

8 cloves **garlic**, sliced

¾ cup **coconut milk**

2⅔ cups **Vegetable Stock** (see page 19)

¼ teaspoon **white pepper**

3 teaspoons **fish sauce** or **light soy sauce**

¼ teaspoon **salt**

½ teaspoon **superfine sugar**

1 large **banana**, peeled and cut obliquely into thin slices

1 large **red chili**, obliquely sliced

TO GARNISH:

fresh **cilantro**

2 **limes**, quartered

scallions, cut into strips

about 3 cups **peanut oil**

8 oz block **ready-fried tofu**, diced

3 cups **water**

1 **lemon grass stalk**

3 **kaffir lime leaves**

1 inch piece of **galangal**, peeled and sliced

1½ teaspoons **salt**

1 teaspoon **superfine sugar**

10 small **green chilies**, chopped

3 tablespoons **lime juice**

1 teaspoon **fish sauce** or **light soy sauce**

2 **scallions**, sliced lengthwise

1 **carrot**, cut into matchsticks

1 **shiitake mushroom**, thinly sliced

handful of fresh **cilantro**, to garnish

15

PREP

20

COOK

4

SERVES

light

Tofu soup

Tofu changes texture considerably when it is deep-fried, and it takes on the flavor from the oil, in this case peanut. This also helps it to hold its shape when added to the soup.

1 Heat the oil in a wok or deep skillet, add the tofu and cook, stirring, for 3 minutes or until golden on all sides. Remove with a slotted spoon and drain on paper towels.

2 Put the measured water, lemon grass, lime leaves, galangal, salt, and sugar in a large saucepan and bring to a boil. Continue to boil for 10 minutes. Remove from the heat.

3 Add the chilies, lime juice, fish or soy sauce, scallions, carrot, and mushroom and simmer for about 4 minutes. Add the tofu and simmer for an additional 2 minutes. Serve hot, garnished with the cilantro.

Hot sour soup with mooli radish

If you don't have any homemade red curry paste prepared, you can make this dish with a bought paste, which is available in most supermarkets. You will see it a lot in Thai recipes, as it forms the base of many soups and curries.

5

PREP

10

COOK

4

SERVES

simple

3 cups **Vegetable Stock** (see page 19)

1 tablespoon **red curry paste**

1 **mooli radish**, peeled and sliced

2 teaspoons **salt**

3 tablespoons **palm sugar** or **light brown sugar**

2 tablespoons **fish sauce** or **light soy sauce**

3 tablespoons **tamarind water**

½ cup **spinach**, leaves and stalks, torn

1 Heat the stock in a large, heavy saucepan. Add the curry paste and stir until well combined. Bring the soup to a boil and add the mooli. Reduce the heat and add the salt, sugar, fish or soy sauce, and tamarind water. Simmer for a few minutes until the mooli slices are tender.

2 Put the spinach in the bottom of a large serving bowl, then pour the hot soup over the top. Serve immediately.

2 tablespoons **sunflower oil**

4 **scallions**, finely chopped

4 **curry leaves** or 1 **bay leaf**

13 oz can chopped **tomatoes**

1 teaspoon **salt**

1 **garlic clove**, crushed

1 teaspoon **black peppercorns**, roughly crushed

3 tablespoons chopped fresh **cilantro**

2 cups **Vegetable Stock** (see page 19)

¾ cup **light cream**

hot crusty **bread**, to serve

PREP

10

20

COOK

4

SERVES

herby

Tomato and cilantro soup

This fragrant tomato soup is infused with plenty of fresh cilantro. Curry leaves give an Indian twist, while the cream thickens and cools it. Garnish with sprigs of cilantro just before serving.

1 Heat the oil in a large, heavy saucepan, add the scallions, curry leaves or bay leaf, and tomatoes and cook over a moderate heat for 2–3 minutes.

2 Add the salt, garlic, crushed peppercorns, cilantro and stock. Stir well and bring to a boil. Reduce the heat, cover, and simmer gently for 10 minutes.

3 Stir in the cream and heat through gently without boiling for 1–2 minutes.

4 Ladle the soup into warm soup bowls and serve immediately with hot crusty bread.

Black bean soup with soba noodles

Soba noodles, a traditional ingredient in Japanese cooking, are made of buckwheat and whole-wheat flour, giving them a nutty flavor but without the dryness of many whole-wheat pastas.

15

PREP

5

COOK

4

SERVES

hearty

1 Cook the soba noodles in a large saucepan of boiling water for about 5 minutes or until just tender.

2 Meanwhile, heat the oil in a large, heavy saucepan, add the scallions and garlic and stir-fry over a moderate heat for 1 minute.

3 Add the chili, ginger, black bean sauce, and stock and bring to a boil. Stir in the bok choy or collard greens, soy sauce, sugar, and peanuts, reduce the heat and simmer gently for 4 minutes.

4 Drain the noodles, then pile them into warm serving bowls. Ladle over the hot soup and serve immediately.

8 oz dried **soba noodles**

2 tablespoons **peanut oil** or **vegetable oil**

1 bunch of **scallions**, sliced

2 **garlic cloves**, roughly chopped

1 **red chili**, seeded, and sliced

1½ inch piece of fresh **gingerroot**, peeled and grated

½ cup **black bean sauce** or **black bean stir-fry sauce**

3 cups **Vegetable Stock** (see page 19)

2 cups shredded **bok choy** or **collard greens**

2 teaspoons **light soy sauce**

1 teaspoon **superfine sugar**

⅓ cup raw, unsalted **shelled peanuts**

3 cups **Vegetable Stock** (see page 19)

2 tablespoons **miso paste**

4 oz **shiitake mushrooms**, sliced

1 cup diced firm **tofu**

crusty **bread**, to serve

5

PREP

8

COOK

4

SERVES

quick

Quick and easy miso soup

This is a very quick and easy recipe, which can be served as an appetizer for a meal or for a light lunch or snack. In restaurants, miso soup is usually sipped straight from the bowl.

1 Pour the stock into a large, heavy saucepan and heat until simmering.

2 Add the miso paste, mushrooms, and tofu and simmer gently for 5 minutes. Serve the soup hot with crusty bread.

Bean sprouts and tofu soup

15*

PREP

10

COOK

4

SERVES

tasty

You can also use ground shrimp instead of chicken or pork, if you prefer. If you are unable to find cilantro roots, use 1 tablespoon finely chopped fresh cilantro leaves instead. Big head bean sprouts are available in most Asian stores.

1 In a bowl, mix together the meat, garlic, cilantro and black fungus.

2 Clean the bean sprouts and discard the tails. Drain the tofu and cut it into roughly 1 inch cubes.

3 Pour the stock into a large, heavy saucepan and bring to a boil. Stir in the soy sauce, then reduce the heat.

4 Shape the meat mixture into small balls. Drop the balls into the simmering stock and cook for 2–3 minutes.

5 Add the tofu and bean sprouts and simmer for an additional 2–3 minutes, taking care not to let the tofu cubes lose their shape. Spoon the soup into a serving bowl and season to taste with pepper. Serve immediately, garnished with the scallions.

5 oz **ground chicken** or **ground pork**

3 **garlic cloves**, finely chopped

2–3 fresh **cilantro roots**, finely chopped

10 dried **black fungus**, soaked in hot water for 20 minutes, drained, and finely chopped

5 oz **big head bean sprouts**

12 oz firm **tofu**

7½ cups **Chicken Stock** (see page 17)

2 tablespoons **light soy sauce**

white pepper

2 **scallions**, thinly sliced, to garnish

* Plus 20 minutes soaking

45 **wonton skins**

6 cups **Chicken Stock**
(see page 17)

8 **Chinese cabbage
leaves**, shredded

2 **scallions**, sliced, to
garnish

STUFFING:

4 oz **ground pork** or
ground chicken

4 oz raw peeled **shrimp**,
roughly chopped

2 **scallions**, thinly sliced

2 slices fresh **gingerroot**,
peeled and finely
chopped

½ cup **bamboo shoots**,
finely chopped

1 **egg white**, lightly
beaten

1 tablespoon **shoyu
sauce** or **tamari sauce**

½ teaspoon **pepper**

1 teaspoon **Chinese rice
wine** or **dry sherry**

1 teaspoon **sesame oil**

1 teaspoon **cornstarch**

20

PREP

10

COOK

6

SERVES

party

Wonton soup

Wontons are small dumplings, which are often served in soup either on their own or with noodles. They are a very popular street food in Asian countries. Wonton skins can be found in the chiller cabinet in Chinese markets and can be frozen, ideally on the day they are bought.

1 Make the stuffing. In a large bowl, mix all the ingredients together.

2 Put about ½ teaspoon of the stuffing in the center of each wonton skin. Brush 2 of the edges of each skin with water, fold over the filling and seal to make a triangle.

3 Bring a large saucepan of water to a boil. Meanwhile, heat the stock in a separate saucepan and add the Chinese cabbage leaves.

4 Gently lower a handful of wontons into the boiling water with a slotted spoon. Stir very gently to separate the wontons and to make sure that they don't stick to the pan bottom.

5 Return the water to a boil and cook the wontons for 5–6 minutes or until they have floated to the surface. Using a slotted spoon, transfer them to a large serving bowl.

6 Pour the stock and Chinese cabbage leaves over the wontons and serve immediately, sprinkled with the scallions.

Tofu in lemon grass fragrant broth

This low-fat yet flavorful soup is very easy to prepare and makes an excellent appetizer for a vegetarian meal.

15

PREP

30

COOK

4

SERVES

fresh

1 Put the stock in a large, heavy saucepan and bring to a boil. Add the lemon grass and red chili. Reduce the heat, cover, and simmer for 15–20 minutes.

2 Add the shoyu or tamari sauce and pepper, then stir in the mushrooms and tofu. Simmer for 5–10 minutes.

3 Add the lime juice, basil leaves, and scallions and stir gently. Serve immediately.

4 cups **Vegetable Stock** (see page 19)

2 **lemon grass stalks**, lightly crushed

1 **red chili**, chopped

2 teaspoons **shoyu sauce** or **tamari sauce**

pinch of **white pepper**

8 oz **closed-cap mushrooms**, chopped

1¼ cups cubed **firm tofu**

juice of ½ **lime**

handful of **basil** leaves

2 **scallions**, sliced lengthwise

8 oz dried **udon noodles**

¾ cup diced firm **tofu**

1 oz dried **wakame seaweed**

4 **scallions**, thinly sliced

6 cups **Vegetable Stock** (see page 19)

3 tablespoons **miso paste**

2 tablespoons **dark soy sauce**

2 tablespoons **mirin**

15

PREP

7

COOK

4

SERVES

light

Japanese miso soup with noodles

This light, healthy soup has a rich flavor. Miso, made from fermented soy bean paste, is a classic ingredient in Japanese cooking, as is wakame seaweed and mirin. Look out for miso and wakame in health food stores and gourmet markets, and mirin in gourmet and Asian markets.

1 Cook the udon noodles in a saucepan of boiling water for 4 minutes. Drain well and transfer to warm soup bowls. Top with the tofu, wakame, and scallions.

2 Meanwhile, put the stock, miso paste, soy sauce, and mirin in a large, heavy saucepan and bring to a boil. Reduce the heat and simmer gently for 3–4 minutes. Pour into the bowls and serve immediately.

Noodle soup with enoki mushrooms

This big-bowl Japanese soup contains just about everything for one meal. Tofu goes well with other Asian ingredients, but you can use shrimp or broiled chicken fillets instead. The strange-looking enoki mushrooms are available in gourmet markets, but if hard to find, use fresh shiitake mushrooms.

1 Heat the oil in a large, nonstick skillet, add the tofu and cook until crisp and golden brown on all sides. Remove with a slotted spoon and drain on paper towels.

2 Meanwhile, put the stock in a large, heavy saucepan and bring to a boil. Reduce the heat, add the vinegar, mirin, and onion and simmer gently for 2 minutes.

3 Cook the udon or egg noodles in a saucepan of boiling water for 1 minute. Drain well and transfer to warm soup bowls. Add the bean sprouts, chili and scallions.

4 Add the mushrooms to the stock and cook for 1 minute. Remove with a slotted spoon and arrange on top of the noodles with the fried tofu. Sprinkle with the fried garlic and cilantro leaves.

5 Stir the miso paste and lime leaves into the stock. Ladle the stock over the ingredients in the bowls and serve piping hot. Serve the soup accompanied with side dishes of soy sauce and crushed red pepper.

15 PREP

6 COOK

4 SERVES

stylish

4 tablespoons **vegetable oil**

1¼ cups cubed firm **tofu**

5 cups **Vegetable Stock** (see page 19)

1 tablespoon **rice wine vinegar**

1 tablespoon **mirin**

1 **sweet white onion**, sliced

8 oz fresh **udon noodles** or **egg noodles**

1¼ cups **bean sprouts**

1 **red chili**, thinly sliced

4 **scallions**, thinly sliced

2 oz **enoki mushrooms**

1 tablespoon **fried garlic**

handful of fresh **cilantro**

2 tablespoons **miso paste**

4 **kaffir lime leaves**, shredded

TO GARNISH:

light soy sauce

crushed red pepper

chilled

2 oz **bread**

⅔ cup **raisins**

⅔ cup **blanched almonds**, toasted

3 tablespoons **olive oil**

3 **garlic cloves**, crushed or roughly chopped

3¾ cups **milk** or **water**

hyssop flowers or **borage flowers**, to garnish

15*

PREP

COOK

6

SERVES

party

Garlic and almond soup

This soup is quite rich and should be served in small quantities. Known in ancient Rome, it has always been considered beneficial to good health, with its antibacterial and heart-protecting properties.

1 Roughly tear the bread into small pieces and put them in a small bowl. Put the raisins in a separate bowl and cover both the bread and raisins with water. Allow to soak for 30–60 minutes or until the raisins are plump.

2 Remove the bread from the water and squeeze to remove the excess moisture. In a blender or food processor, blend the bread with the almonds to form a smooth paste.

3 Add the oil, garlic, raisins, and milk or water and blend again until smooth.

4 Cover the soup and chill in the refrigerator for 2–3 hours to allow the flavors to mingle. Serve in small soup bowls topped with hyssop or borage flowers.

* Plus 2½–4 hours soaking and chilling

Vichyssoise

15* PREP

40 COOK

This well-known French-sounding soup was actually created in the USA, and although the name is usually used for chilled leek and potato soups thickened with cream, the basic recipe can be successfully adapted to other vegetables, such as zucchini.

1 Slice off the green tops of the leeks and set aside for use in another recipe. Slice the white parts of the leeks thinly.

2 Melt the butter in a large, heavy saucepan, add the leeks and onion and cook over a moderate heat for 5 minutes or until softened but not browned.

3 Add the stock, nutmeg, and potatoes and season to taste with salt and pepper. Bring to a boil. Reduce the heat, partially cover the pan and simmer for 25 minutes. Pour in the milk and simmer for an additional 5–8 minutes. Allow to cool slightly.

4 In a blender or food processor, blend the soup in batches until smooth, then rub it through a sieve into a bowl. Add the light cream, stir well, and cover closely. Chill in the refrigerator for at least 3 hours. Just before serving, swirl in the heavy cream. Taste and adjust the seasoning if necessary. Serve in chilled bowls, garnishing each portion with a generous sprinkling of snipped chives.

6 SERVES

classic

2 lb **leeks**

¼ cup **butter**

1 **onion**, chopped

4 cups **Vegetable Stock** (see page 19)

pinch of **grated nutmeg**

1½ lb old **potatoes**, diced

2½ cups **milk**

1¼ cups **light cream**

⅔ cup **heavy cream**, chilled

salt and **white pepper**

2 tablespoons snipped **chives**, to garnish

* Plus 3 hours chilling

¼ cup **butter**

1 **onion**, chopped

1 lb **carrots**, sliced

1½ cups sliced **leeks**, white parts only

2½ cups **water**

2½ cups **Vegetable Stock** (see page 19)

1 teaspoon chopped fresh **cilantro**

⅔ cup **heavy cream**, chilled

salt and **pepper**

finely chopped **parsley** or fresh **cilantro**, to garnish

PREP

COOK

SERVES

stylish

Carrot vichyssoise

Winter vegetables are used in this version of the traditional Vichyssoise, which is finished with fresh herbs. To chill the bowls, simply place them in the refrigerator with the soup.

1 Melt the butter in a large, heavy saucepan, add the onion and cook over a moderate heat for 5 minutes or until softened but not browned. Add the carrots and leeks and cook, stirring, for 2–3 minutes. Add, the measured water, stock, and cilantro. Season to taste with salt.

2 Bring to a boil, then reduce the heat, cover, and simmer for 30–35 minutes until the vegetables are tender. Allow to cool slightly.

3 In a blender or food processor, blend the soup in batches until smooth, then transfer it to a bowl. Cover closely. Chill in the refrigerator for at least 3 hours. Just before serving, stir in the chilled cream. Serve in chilled soup bowls and sprinkle each portion with finely chopped parsley or cilantro to garnish.

* Plus 3 hours chilling

Shrimp vichyssoise

Shrimp work well in chilled soups because they taste equally good hot or cold. You could add a couple of cooked, unpeeled shrimp to the side of each bowl.

15* PREP

40 COOK

6 SERVES

rich

2 lb **leeks**

¼ cup **butter**

1 **onion**, chopped

4 cups **Vegetable Stock** (see page 19)

pinch of **grated nutmeg**

1½ lb old **potatoes**, diced

2½ cups **milk**

1¼ cups **light cream**

6 oz cooked peeled **shrimp**, plus extra to garnish

⅔ cup **heavy cream**, chilled

salt and **white pepper**

1 Slice off the green tops of the leeks and set aside for use in another recipe. Slice the white parts of the leeks thinly.

2 Melt the butter in a large, heavy saucepan, add the leeks and onion and cook over a moderate heat for 5 minutes or until softened but not browned.

3 Add the stock, nutmeg, and potatoes and season to taste with salt and pepper. Bring to a boil. Reduce the heat, partially cover, and simmer for 25 minutes. Pour in the milk and simmer for an additional 5–8 minutes. Allow to cool slightly.

4 In a blender or food processor, blend the soup in batches until smooth, then rub it through a sieve into a bowl. Add the light cream and shrimp, stir well, and cover closely. Chill in the refrigerator for at least 3 hours. Just before serving, swirl in the heavy cream. Taste and adjust the seasoning if necessary. Serve in chilled bowls, garnishing each portion with a few extra shrimp.

* Plus 3 hours chilling

4 slices of day-old **bread**, crusts removed

⅔ cup **blanched almonds**, roughly chopped

1–2 **garlic cloves**, chopped

½ cup extra virgin **olive oil**

2–3 tablespoons **sherry vinegar**

4 cups iced **water**

salt

1½ cups **white seeded grapes**, to garnish

15*

PREP

COOK

4

SERVES

light

White gazpacho

Bread and almonds form the basis of this creamy colored soup, which is based on the Spanish original. The consistency should be thin, as this is a light summer dish.

1 Put the bread in a bowl, cover with cold water and allow to soak for 5 minutes. Remove from the water and squeeze to remove the excess moisture.

2 In a blender or food processor, blend the the almonds and garlic until very finely ground and almost paste-like. With the motor running, gradually add the bread and blend until smooth, then gradually add the oil in a thin, steady stream. When the oil has been incorporated, add the vinegar, scraping down the sides of the bowl if necessary. Pour in 1¼ cups of the measured iced water and blend briefly to combine.

3 Strain through a sieve into a large bowl, pressing with the back of a ladle to extract as much liquid as possible. Stir in the remaining iced water to make a thin soup. Season to taste with salt. Cover closely and chill in the refrigerator for at least 3 hours.

4 Just before serving, stir the soup well. Ladle into individual chilled bowls and serve garnished with a few grapes.

* Plus 3 hours chilling

Beet gazpacho

This stunning, deep-pink soup is even better if it's allowed to infuse and chill for an hour before serving. It makes a perfect no-fuss appetizer for entertaining because you can prepare it in advance and simply serve it when you and your guests are ready to eat.

1 In a blender or food processor, blend the beet, onion, garlic, tomatoes, capers, and cornichons until smooth.

2 Add the bread crumbs and blend, then gradually blend in the stock, oil, and vinegar to form a smooth soup. Season to taste with salt and pepper.

3 Serve the soup in chilled soup bowls, topped with a spoonful of crème fraîche and some chopped dill, and sprinkled with pepper.

15*

PREP

COOK

4

SERVES

easy

1 lb cooked **beet in natural juices**, drained and chopped

1 small **onion**, roughly chopped

2 **garlic cloves**, roughly chopped

2 **tomatoes**, roughly chopped

2 tablespoons **capers**, drained

4 baby **cornichons**, drained and chopped

¼ cup dry **bread crumbs**

2½ cups **Vegetable Stock** (see page 19)

⅔ cup extra virgin **olive oil**

2 tablespoons **white wine vinegar**

salt and **pepper**

TO SERVE:

crème fraîche

chopped **dill**

* Plus 3 hours chilling

1 **red bell pepper**, cored, seeded, and roughly chopped

1 **green bell pepper**, cored, seeded, and roughly chopped

3 lb **tomatoes**, skinned and roughly chopped

2 **garlic cloves**, crushed

1 slice of day-old **bread**, crusts removed

5 tablespoons **olive oil**

6 tablespoons **white wine vinegar**

1 teaspoon golden **superfine sugar**

6 tablespoons **water**

6–8 **ice cubes**, plus extra to serve

TO SERVE:

1 **red bell pepper**, cored, seeded, and finely diced

1 **green bell pepper**, cored, seeded, and finely diced

1 small **cucumber**, finely diced

1 **red onion**, finely diced

flat leaf parsley leaves

20 *

PREP

COOK

6

SERVES

fresh

Gazpacho with raw salsa

This colorful and wonderfully refreshing soup, made with sweet peppers and tomatoes, is packed with flavor and vitality.

1 In a blender or food processor, blend the red and green peppers, tomatoes, and garlic to form a fairly smooth paste.

2 Roughly tear the bread into small pieces and add to the tomato mixture with the oil, vinegar, and sugar. Add the measured water and blend until smooth. Add the ice cubes, then cover, and chill in the refrigerator for at least 1 hour.

3 Serve the chilled soup with extra ice cubes and topped with the diced peppers, cucumber, red onion, and parsley leaves.

* Plus 1 hour chilling

Gazpacho and almond soup

25*

PREP

COOK

6

SERVES

tasty

Gazpacho is the classic cold vegetable soup of Spain, with as many different recipes as there are towns. This version is thickened with almonds, but you could use dry or fresh bread crumbs instead. Reserve some of the diced vegetables to garnish.

1 Remove the cores from the tomatoes with a small, sharp knife. Plunge them into boiling water for 5–10 seconds, then remove and refresh in cold water. Slip off the skins and discard. Cut in half around the center and gently squeeze out and discard the seeds. Dice the flesh.

2 In a blender or food processor, blend the diced tomatoes, onion, garlic, bell peppers, cucumber, chilies, olives, and capers until fairly smooth. Add the ground almonds and blend again to thicken.

3 Transfer the mixture to a bowl and stir in the vinegar, sugar, cold stock, tomato juice, and oil. Cover and chill in the refrigerator for at least 1 hour, then stir in the herbs. Season to taste with salt and pepper. Serve in chilled soup bowls.

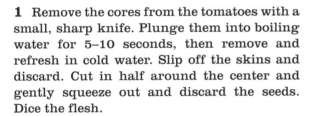

2 lb vine-ripened **tomatoes**

1 **red onion**, chopped

4 **garlic cloves**

2 **green bell peppers** or **red bell peppers**, cored, seeded, and chopped

½ **cucumber**, peeled and chopped

2 **red chilies**, seeded and chopped

3 tablespoons pitted **green olives**, chopped

1 tablespoon **capers**

½ cup **ground almonds**, toasted

3 tablespoons **red wine vinegar**

1 tablespoon **sugar**

1¾ cups cold **Vegetable Stock** (see page 19)

⅔ cup **tomato juice**

⅔ cup extra virgin **olive oil**

2 tablespoons chopped **parsley**

2 tablespoons chopped fresh **cilantro**

salt and **pepper**

* Plus 1 hour chilling

1 small **red onion**, chopped

2 **garlic cloves**, chopped

1 inch piece of fresh **gingerroot**, peeled and grated

1 small **red bell pepper**, cored, seeded, and chopped

2 **red chilies**, seeded, and chopped

1 lb ripe **tomatoes**, chopped

2 tablespoons chopped fresh **cilantro**

4 **poppadums**, crumbled

1¼ cups cold **Vegetable Stock** (see page 19)

1¼ cups **tomato juice**

4 tablespoons extra virgin **olive oil**

2 tablespoons **white wine vinegar**

salt and **pepper**

TO GARNISH:

plain yogurt

poppadums

sprigs of fresh **cilantro**

20*

PREP

COOK

4

SERVES

spicy

Gazpacho with Indian flavors

A classic Spanish gazpacho is given an exotic twist with the addition of Indian spices and poppadums to make a refreshing soup for a hot summer's day.

1 In a blender or food processor, blend the onion, garlic, ginger, red bell pepper, chilies, tomatoes, cilantro, and crumbled poppadums until smooth.

2 Transfer the mixture to a bowl and stir in the remaining ingredients. Season to taste with salt and pepper. Cover closely and freeze for at least 15 minutes until well chilled.

3 Spoon the gazpacho into chilled soup bowls and serve garnished with yogurt, poppadums, and cilantro sprigs.

* Plus 15 minutes freezing

Chilled borscht with apple

15*
PREP

40
COOK

Beet has an amazing color and is packed with iron, beta-carotene, and folic acid. Here it teams well with apple in an adaptation of the traditional Russian soup. You can add chilled sour cream or a spoonful of plain yogurt just before serving.

1 Peel the beet and cut the flesh into thin matchstick strips.

2 Trim the fennel and cut the bulb into strips. Put the beet and fennel in a large, heavy saucepan with the measured water and bring slowly to a boil. Reduce the heat, cover, and simmer gently for 20–30 minutes or until the vegetables are tender.

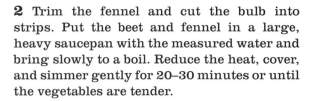

4
SERVES

stylish

3 Add the apple juice and thyme leaves and season to taste with salt and pepper. Simmer for an additional 10 minutes. Remove from the heat and stir in the lemon juice and chives. Taste and adjust the seasoning if necessary.

4 Allow the soup to cool, then pour it into a bowl, cover closely, and chill in the refrigerator for at least 3 hours. Ladle into chilled bowls and serve with soda bread.

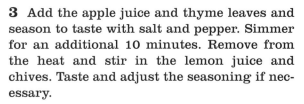

1 lb raw **beet**

1 small **fennel bulb**

2½ cups **water**

2½ cups **apple juice**

1 teaspoon **thyme leaves**

4 tablespoons **lemon juice**

1 tablespoon snipped **chives**

salt and **pepper**

soda bread, to serve

* Plus 3 hours chilling

2 **onions**, chopped

2 **carrots**, chopped

3 sprigs of **parsley**

6 **black peppercorns**

1 **bay leaf**

4 cups **water**

4 cooked peeled **beets**, grated

1 **sugar cube** or
1 teaspoon **superfine sugar**

2 teaspoons **white wine vinegar**

1½ teaspoons **granulated gelatin**

salt

TO GARNISH:

⅔ cup **sour cream**

1 teaspoon mild **curry powder**

snipped **chives**

20*

PREP

90

COOK

4

SERVES

fresh

Chilled beet soup

Beet's distinctive red juice is something to be wary of when preparing the vegetable, as it readily stains. So take care to protect both your hands and clothes.

1 Put the onions, carrots, parsley, peppercorns, and bay leaf in a large, heavy saucepan, add the measured water and bring to a boil. Reduce the heat, cover, and simmer for 1 hour or until the vegetables are tender.

2 Strain the stock through a sieve into the bowl containing the beet and mix well, discarding the solids in the sieve. Transfer the beet and stock to a clean saucepan and add the sugar and vinegar. Season to taste with salt. Simmer gently for 10 minutes without boiling. Strain into a clean saucepan, discarding the beets.

3 Spoon 2 tablespoons of the hot soup into a cup or pitcher. Add the gelatin and stir until thoroughly dissolved. Stir the mixture into the pan. Allow to cool, then pour into a bowl, cover closely, and chill in the refrigerator for at least 3 hours or until set.

4 In a small bowl, mix the sour cream with the curry powder. Break up the soup and serve in chilled bowls, garnished with the sour cream mixture and snipped chives.

* Plus 3 hours chilling

Iced tomato soup with salsa verde

This soup relies on full-flavored, sun-ripened tomatoes to conjure up the taste of southern Italy. Adding the salsa verde gives the soup a sweet and sour flavor, popular in the south of Italy and Sicily. The salsa will keep for up to a week in the refrigerator.

25*

PREP

COOK

6

SERVES

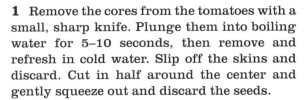

party

1 Remove the cores from the tomatoes with a small, sharp knife. Plunge them into boiling water for 5–10 seconds, then remove and refresh in cold water. Slip off the skins and discard. Cut in half around the center and gently squeeze out and discard the seeds.

2 Core and seed the bell peppers, then roughly chop. Seed the chili and finely chop. In a blender or food processor, blend the tomatoes, chili, and garlic to a rough puree. Transfer to a bowl and stir in the tomatoes, oil and vinegar. Season to taste with salt and pepper. Cover closely and chill overnight.

3 Meanwhile, make the salsa verde. Put 1 teaspoon salt and the garlic in a mortar and pound with a pestle until creamy. Transfer to a bowl and stir in the anchovies, herbs, capers, oil, and lemon juice. Season to taste with pepper. Transfer to a jar and pour a layer of oil on top to exclude the air.

4 Stir the crushed ice into the soup and serve in chilled soup bowls, with the salsa verde separately in a bowl to stir into the soup.

2 lb vine-ripened **tomatoes**

2 large **red bell peppers**

1 small **red chili**

2 **garlic cloves**, chopped

2½ cups **passata** (pureed tomatoes)

6 tablespoons extra virgin **olive oil**

2 tablespoons **balsamic vinegar** (or to taste)

salt and **pepper**

2½ cups **crushed ice**, to serve

SALSA VERDE:

2 **garlic cloves**, finely chopped

4 **anchovy fillets** in oil, rinsed and chopped

3 tablespoons chopped **parsley**

3 tablespoons chopped **mint**

3 tablespoons chopped **basil**

2 tablespoons **capers**

⅔ cup extra virgin **olive oil**, plus extra to seal

2 tablespoons **lemon juice**

* Plus overnight chilling

2 tablespoons **butter**

2 tablespoons **olive oil**

1 large **onion**, chopped

1 **garlic clove**, chopped

about 2 lb **tomatoes**, skinned and roughly chopped

4 cups **Chicken Stock** (see page 17)

1 teaspoon chopped **oregano**

1½ teaspoons **superfine sugar**

¼ teaspoon **celery salt**

pinch of **grated nutmeg**

1 tablespoon **Worcestershire sauce**

⅔ cup **sour cream**

salt and **pepper**

TO GARNISH:

6 **Spanish olives**, pitted

chopped **parsley**

20* PREP

55 COOK

6 SERVES

classic

Chilled tomato soup

This light, tasty soup is an ideal appetizer for a summer lunch. Replace the chicken stock with homemade vegetable stock if you are cooking for vegetarians.

1 Melt the butter with the oil in a large, heavy saucepan, add the onion and garlic and cook over a moderate heat for 5 minutes or until softened but not browned. Add the tomatoes and cook, stirring, for 3 minutes.

2 Add the stock, oregano, sugar, celery salt, nutmeg, and Worcestershire sauce. Season to taste with salt and pepper. Stir well and bring to a boil, reduce the heat, partially cover, and simmer for 45 minutes. Allow to cool a little.

3 In a blender or food processor, blend the soup in batches, then transfer it to a bowl. Stir in the sour cream and allow the soup to cool completely. Cover the bowl closely and chill in the refrigerator for at least 3 hours.

4 Meanwhile, put an olive in each section of a 6-cube ice-cube tray and top with cold water. Freeze until solid. Serve the soup in chilled bowls, each portion garnished with an olive ice cube and a sprinkling of chopped parsley.

* Plus 3 hours chilling

Chilled yogurt, cucumber, and mint soup

Cool and refreshing yogurt soup, spiced with cumin and chili, makes a gentle start to a spicy Indian meal. It has a slightly sharp, piquant flavor, and the addition of finely chopped cucumber and tomato gives it a lovely bite.

1 In a blender or food processor, blend the yogurt, stock, ginger, cumin, and chili powder until smooth. Transfer to a bowl.

2 Add the cucumber, tomatoes, and mint to the yogurt mixture. Season to taste with salt and pepper and stir to combine.

3 Cover closely and chill in the refrigerator for 30 minutes. To serve, ladle the soup into chilled bowls, drizzle over a little extra yogurt, and sprinkle with some roasted cumin seeds to garnish.

15 *

PREP

COOK

4

SERVES

light

3 cups **plain yogurt**, plus extra to serve

3 cups **Vegetable Stock** (see page 19)

½ teaspoon finely grated fresh **gingerroot**

½ teaspoon **ground cumin**

¼ teaspoon **chili powder**

1 small **cucumber**, finely diced

2 **plum tomatoes**, seeded and diced

4 tablespoons finely chopped **mint**

salt and **pepper**

roasted **cumin seeds**, to garnish

¼ cup **butter**

2 bunches of **watercress**, stalks discarded, roughly chopped, plus extra leaves to garnish

4 cups **Vegetable Stock** (see page 19)

2 cups chopped **potatoes**

pinch of **grated nutmeg**

salt and **pepper**

TO GARNISH:

⅔ cup **light cream**, chilled

1 tablespoon **olive oil** (optional)

10*

PREP

25

COOK

Chilled watercress soup

One of the great advantages of serving chilled soups is that they can be prepared in advance and kept in the refrigerator until you're ready to eat. And in addition, no reheating is required!

4

SERVES

stylish

1 Melt the butter in a large, heavy saucepan, add the watercress and cook over a moderate heat, stirring, for 3 minutes. Add the stock, potatoes, and nutmeg. Season to taste with pepper. Bring to a boil, then reduce the heat, cover, and simmer for 15–20 minutes or until the potatoes are tender. Allow to cool.

2 In a blender or food processor, blend the soup in batches until smooth, then transfer it to a large bowl. Cover closely and chill in the refrigerator for at least 3 hours.

3 Just before serving, fold in the chilled cream. Taste and add salt if necessary. Serve in chilled bowls, garnishing each portion with a few watercress leaves, pepper, and a drizzle of olive oil, if desired.

* Plus 3 hours chilling

Chilled lettuce and dill soup

10***
PREP

Dill is a delicate herb with a distinctive flavor, and it's perfect for this summer soup. The light, fresh taste of the lettuce makes this ideal for alfresco eating.

25
COOK

1 Melt the butter in a large, heavy saucepan, add the onion and cook over a moderate heat for about 5 minutes or until softened. Add the flour and cook, stirring constantly, for 2 minutes. Beat in the stock and bring to a boil, beating constantly.

4
SERVES

2 Add the lettuce, 2 tablespoons of the dill and the nutmeg. Reduce the heat, cover, and simmer, stirring occasionally, for about 15 minutes. Allow to cool.

herby

3 In a blender or food processor, blend the soup in batches, then transfer it to a bowl. Stir in the lemon juice and pepper, and season to taste with salt. Cover closely and chill in the refrigerator for at least 3 hours.

4 In a small bowl, mix the remaining dill with the cream. Serve the soup in chilled bowls, garnishing each portion with a swirl of the cream and dill mixture.

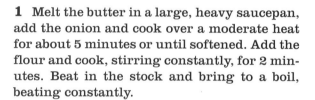

¼ cup **butter**

1 small **onion**, chopped

1 tablespoon **all-purpose flour**

4 cups **Vegetable Stock** (see page 19)

outer leaves of 2 **butterhead lettuces**, roughly shredded

3 tablespoons chopped **dill**

pinch of **grated nutmeg**

1 tablespoon **lemon juice**

¼–½ teaspoon **white pepper**

salt

4 tablespoons **heavy cream**, to garnish

* Plus 3 hours chilling

5 **potatoes**, diced

3 **onions**, sliced

15 oz can **cream of mushroom soup**

2 tablespoons **butter**

4 cups **milk**

1 teaspoon **English mustard**

salt and **pepper**

TO GARNISH:

2 tablespoons **cottage cheese**

few snipped **chives**

paprika

PREP

COOK

SERVES

Chilled potato chowder

We tend to think of chowders as being winter soups, but this recipe proves that they taste just as good when chilled. The soup is rubbed through a sieve rather then being blended so that it retains a pleasantly coarse texture.

1 Put the potatoes and onions in a large saucepan, add just enough water to cover and bring to a boil. Reduce the heat and simmer for 15 minutes, or until tender. Drain and rub the mixture through a coarse sieve into a clean saucepan.

2 Add the soup, butter, milk, and mustard. Season to taste with salt and pepper and stir to mix. Heat gently until the soup begins to simmer. Pour into a bowl and allow to cool. Cover closely and chill in the refrigerator for at least 3 hours.

3 Serve the soup in chilled bowls, garnishing each portion with a little cottage cheese, a few snipped chives, and a dusting of paprika.

* Plus 3 hours chilling

Chilled avocado soup

10*

PREP

COOK

This delicately flavored, easy-to-prepare soup must not be left for longer than 1 hour before it is served or it will lose its pale green color. Make sure that all ingredients are chilled.

4

SERVES

quick

1 Cut the avocados in half and remove and discard the pits. Peel the flesh and slice it into a blender or food processor, discarding any discolored flesh.

2 Add the lemon juice, yogurt, and 2½ cups of the stock and blend the mixture to a smooth puree. Transfer to a bowl.

3 Beat in the chilled cream, then add the remaining stock, cayenne pepper, and pepper. Season to taste with salt. Stir well, cover closely, and chill in the refrigerator for 1 hour.

4 Serve the soup in chilled bowls, sprinkling each portion with snipped chives to garnish.

2 large ripe **avocados**

1 teaspoon **lemon juice**

⅔ cup **plain yogurt**

3 cups **Chicken Stock** (see page 17), chilled

4 tablespoons **light cream**, chilled

cayenne pepper

¼ teaspoon **white pepper**

salt

2 tablespoons snipped **chives**, to garnish

* Plus 1 hour chilling

6 **celery sticks**, about 8oz

5 cups **Vegetable Stock** (see page 19)

1 **onion**, chopped

2 cups diced **potatoes**

1 teaspoon **ground cumin**

3 tablespoons chilled **sour cream**

salt

finely chopped **celery leaves**, to garnish

15*

PREP

25

COOK

4

SERVES

simple

Chilled celery soup with cumin

An unusual combination! The cumin gives a touch of aromatic flavor to the subtle taste of the celery.

1 Thinly slice enough celery to yield 2 tablespoons. Set aside in a small bowl. Grate the remaining celery.

2 Combine the grated celery, stock, onion, potatoes, and cumin in a large, heavy saucepan. Season to taste with salt. Bring to a boil, then reduce the heat, partially cover, and cook for 20–25 minutes.

3 In a blender or food processor, blend the soup in batches until smooth, then transfer it to a bowl. Add the reserved sliced celery and stir well. Allow to cool. Cover closely and chill in the refrigerator for at least 3 hours.

4 Just before serving, stir in the sour cream. Serve in chilled bowls, garnished with finely chopped celery leaves.

* Plus 3 hours chilling

Chilled zucchini soup

15*

PREP

This is the perfect soup for a light lunch. Zucchini and potatoes are flavored with fresh ginger and a hint of nutmeg. A dash of cream finishes the dish.

55

COOK

1 Cut off the ends of the zucchini and slice thickly into a colander. Sprinkle with salt and allow to drain for 10–15 minutes. Rinse under cold running water, drain thoroughly and pat dry with paper towels.

6

SERVES

2 Melt the butter in a large, heavy saucepan, add the onions and cook over a moderate heat for 5 minutes or until softened but not browned. Add the zucchini and cook over a low heat, stirring frequently, for 5 minutes.

thick

3 Add the stock, ginger, and nutmeg. Season to taste with pepper. Bring to a boil and add the potatoes. Reduce the heat, partially cover, and simmer for 40–45 minutes or until the vegetables are very tender.

4 In a blender or food processor, blend the soup in batches until smooth, then transfer to a bowl. Allow to cool, then cover closely, and chill in the refrigerator for at least 3 hours.

5 Serve in chilled bowls, garnishing each portion with a swirl of chilled cream.

* Plus 10–15 minutes draining and 3 hours chilling

3 lb small **zucchini**

¼ cup **butter**

1 cup chopped **onions**

4 cups **Vegetable Stock** (see page 19)

1 tablespoon grated fresh **gingerroot**

pinch of **grated nutmeg**

3 cups diced **potatoes**

salt and **pepper**

⅔ cup **light cream**, chilled, to garnish

¼ cup **butter**

1 small **onion**, chopped

5 cups frozen **peas**

¼ teaspoon **superfine sugar**

5 cups **Vegetable Stock** (see page 19)

4 tablespoons chopped **mint**

2½ cups roughly chopped **potatoes**

⅔ cup **heavy cream**

salt and **white pepper**

10[*]

PREP

35

COOK

6

SERVES

herby

Chilled pea soup with mint

Peas and mint are the perfect match for a summer soup, and this chilled version of a classic soup is wonderfully refreshing. You can use freshly shelled peas if you prefer.

1 Melt the butter in a large, heavy saucepan, add the onion and cook over a moderate heat for about 5 minutes or until softened but not browned.

2 Add the peas, sugar, stock, and 3 tablespoons of the mint. Season to taste with pepper. Stir well and bring to a boil. Add the potatoes, then reduce the heat, partially cover, and simmer for 20–25 minutes.

3 In a blender or food processor, blend the soup in batches until smooth, then transfer it to a clean saucepan. Taste and adjust the seasoning if necessary, add the cream and stir well. Heat gently without boiling. Allow to cool, then cover closely, and chill in the refrigerator for at least 3 hours.

4 Serve in chilled bowls, garnishing each portion with some of the remaining chopped mint.

* Plus 3 hours chilling

Chilled cucumber and pepper soup

This impressive-looking soup uses crunchy bell pepper and cucumber as a garnish. If you're preparing the soup in advance, wait until you're ready to serve before preparing the garnish ingredients because they should be as fresh as possible.

1 Cut one-third of one of the cucumbers into fine dice and reserve for the garnish. Chop the remaining cucumbers roughly.

2 In a blender or food processor, blend the chopped cucumber and garlic until very smooth. Pour into a bowl and mix with the yogurt. Add enough of the measured iced water to make a smooth soup. Season to taste with salt and pepper and stir in the mint. Cover and chill in the refrigerator for 4 hours.

3 Chop 1 yellow pepper into fine dice, mix with the reserved cucumber and set aside for garnish. Chop the remaining pepper. Put in a small saucepan with the lime or lemon juice, sugar, measured water, and cayenne pepper. Bring to a boil, reduce the heat and simmer for 10–15 minutes until tender and the liquid has reduced. In a blender or food processor, blend until smooth. Strain through a sieve into a bowl. Allow to cool, cover, and chill in the refrigerator for 4 hours.

4 Serve in bowls, sprinkled with the pepper and cucumber. Drizzle over the pepper puree.

30* PREP

15 COOK

4 SERVES

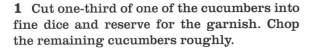

party

* Plus 4 hours chilling

2 **cucumbers**, peeled and seeded

1 **garlic clove**, crushed

1 cup **plain yogurt**, preferably Greek

about ⅓ cup iced **water**

4 tablespoons chopped **mint**

2 **yellow bell peppers**, cored and seeded

2 tablespoons **lime juice** or **lemon juice**

1 tablespoon **superfine sugar**

⅓ cup **water**

pinch of **cayenne pepper**

salt and **pepper**

½ teaspoon **salt**

1¼ cups **water**

10 oz **asparagus**

1 tablespoon **peanut oil**

1 **garlic clove**, finely chopped

1 **shallot**, sliced

½ teaspoon **red pepper flakes**

½ teaspoon **white pepper**

1¼ cups **coconut milk**

1 tablespoon **fish sauce** or **light soy sauce**

10*

PREP

20

COOK

4

SERVES

posh

Khun Tom's chilled asparagus

The coconut milk adds a touch of sweetness to this delicious asparagus soup, and dried chilies give the whole dish a lift. It's very quick and easy to prepare, but looks fantastic when served.

1 Put the salt and measured water in a large saucepan and bring to a boil. Add the asparagus and cook for 10–12 minutes until tender. Drain and reserve the water. Cut the tips off the asparagus and reserve for garnish. In a blender or food processor, blend the remaining asparagus and its liquid until smooth. Set aside.

2 Heat the oil in a large, heavy saucepan, add the garlic, shallot, chilies, and pepper and cook over a moderate heat, stirring, for 1 minute. Add the puréed asparagus. Bring to a boil and add the coconut milk. Boil for 2 minutes, then add the fish or soy sauce. Allow to cool, then cover, and chill in the refrigerator for 4 hours.

3 Serve in chilled soup bowls, garnished with the reserved asparagus tips.

* Plus 4 hours chilling

Chilled spinach soup

15* PREP

20 COOK

4 SERVES

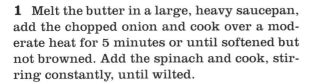

rich

The vibrant color and rich, creamy flavor of this soup will make it an instant favorite. The sour cream makes it quite rich, so you only need a small amount of soup—perfect for an appetizer.

1 Melt the butter in a large, heavy saucepan, add the chopped onion and cook over a moderate heat for 5 minutes or until softened but not browned. Add the spinach and cook, stirring constantly, until wilted.

2 Stir in the stock, potatoes, lemon juice, nutmeg, and salt and pepper to taste. Bring to a boil, then reduce the heat, partially cover, and simmer for 10–12 minutes or until the potatoes are tender.

3 In a blender or food processor, blend the soup in batches until smooth, transferring to a bowl. Leave to cool, then cover, and chill in the refrigerator for at least 3 hours.

4 In a small bowl, blend the sour cream with the grated onion and cucumber. Serve the soup in chilled bowls, each portion topped with a little of the sour cream mixture.

¼ cup **butter**

1 **onion**, chopped

1 lb fresh or frozen **spinach**

5 cups **Vegetable Stock** (see page 19)

8 oz **potatoes**, thinly sliced

1 teaspoon **lemon juice**

pinch of **grated nutmeg**

salt and **white pepper**

TO GARNISH:

⅔ cup **sour cream**

1 teaspoon finely grated **onion**

2 tablespoons peeled and diced **cucumber**

* Plus 3 hours chilling

1 large **cucumber**

⅔ cup **plain yogurt**

⅔ cup **sour cream**

½ cup **milk**

¼ teaspoon **superfine sugar**

¼ teaspoon **white pepper**

¼ teaspoon **Tabasco sauce**

8 oz cooked peeled **shrimp**, thawed if frozen

1 tablespoon finely chopped **mint**

1 tablespoon snipped **chives**

1 tablespoon chopped **dill**

salt

TO GARNISH:

4 small sprigs of **mint**

paprika, for dusting

10*

PREP

COOK

4

SERVES

herby

Chilled shrimp and yogurt soup

This tangy, refreshing soup relies on the addition of really fresh herbs for its fragrant flavor and attractive color.

1 Peel the cucumber. Cut it in half, remove and discard the seeds, then cut all the flesh into small dice. Put it in a sieve or colander, sprinkle with salt and allow to drain for 20 minutes. Rinse under cold running water, then drain thoroughly and pat dry with paper towels.

2 In a blender or food processor, blend together the yogurt, sour cream, milk, sugar, pepper, and Tabasco sauce. Pour into a bowl and season to taste with salt.

3 Stir in the shrimp, mint, chives, and dill, then add the cucumber. Mix well, cover closely, and chill in the refrigerator for at least 2 hours.

4 Serve the soup in chilled bowls, each portion garnished with a mint sprig and a dusting of paprika.

* Plus 20 minutes draining and 2 hours chilling

Chilled shrimp and pea soup

20*

PREP

The shells of the shrimp are full of flavor, which is why they're used here to infuse the stock. You can serve the soup with crisp whole-wheat toast for dunking.

30

COOK

1 Shell the peas if using fresh, reserving the pods. Peel the shrimp, reserving the shells. Cover the shrimp and refrigerate. Put the shrimp shells and pea pods in a large, heavy saucepan with the onion, garlic, and stock or water. Bring to a boil, then reduce the heat and simmer gently for 15 minutes.

2 Strain the liquid into a clean saucepan, add the peas and nutmeg and season to taste with salt and pepper. Return to a boil, then reduce the heat and simmer until the peas are tender. In a blender or food processor, blend the soup in batches until smooth.

3 Pour the soup into a bowl and taste and adjust the seasoning if necessary. Stir in the wine (if using), sour cream, and lemon juice. Allow to cool, then cover and chill in the refrigerator for at least 2 hours.

4 Pour the soup into individual soup bowls and divide the shrimp equally between them. Add an extra spoonful of sour cream to each bowl and a little salmon roe, if desired, and sprinkle with chives.

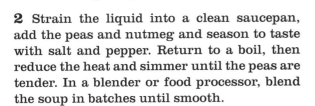

4

SERVES

stylish

2½ cups **peas**, thawed if frozen

8 oz cooked small **shrimp**, unpeeled

1 **onion**, chopped

1 **garlic clove**, crushed

2½ cups **Chicken Stock** (see page 17) or **water**

pinch of **grated nutmeg**

⅔ cup **dry white wine** (optional)

⅔ cup **sour cream**, plus extra to serve (optional)

1 tablespoon **lemon juice**

salt and **pepper**

TO SERVE:

4 teaspoons **salmon roe** (optional)

2 tablespoons snipped **chives**

* Plus 2 hours chilling

¼ cup **butter**

1 **onion**, chopped

1 **garlic clove**, finely chopped

8 oz **smoked salmon**, finely chopped

3 tablespoons **all-purpose flour**

4 cups **Chicken Stock** (see page 17)

1 tablespoon **lemon juice**

1 **bay leaf**

¼ teaspoon **paprika**

⅔ cup **light cream**

4 oz cooked peeled **shrimp**, thawed if frozen

1 teaspoon **dill**, chopped

salt and **white pepper**

6 sprigs of **dill**, to garnish

15*

PREP

20

COOK

6

SERVES

posh

Chilled cream of smoked salmon soup

Dill goes well with smoked salmon, and the addition of lemon juice adds a piquant edge to this sophisticated recipe.

1 Melt the butter in a large, heavy saucepan, add the onion and garlic and cook over a moderate heat for 1 minute. Add the salmon and cook, stirring, for 1 minute. Sprinkle with the flour and cook, stirring constantly, for 30 seconds. Gradually pour in the stock, stirring constantly. Bring to a boil, stirring constantly. Reduce the heat and simmer for 5 minutes.

2 Add the lemon juice, bay leaf, and paprika. Season with salt and pepper. Simmer for 5–8 minutes. Remove from the heat and allow to cool. Remove and discard the bay leaf.

3 In a blender or food processor, blend the soup in batches until smooth. Strain through a coarse sieve into a bowl. Stir in the cream, shrimp, and chopped dill. Allow to cool, then cover closely, and chill in the refrigerator for 3–4 hours or overnight.

4 Serve the soup in chilled bowls, garnishing each portion with a dill sprig.

* Plus 3–4 hours or overnight chilling

Melon and prosciutto soup

A favorite Italian appetizer is transformed into a soup in this quick and simple recipe. The key is to use good-quality ingredients. Serve in wine glasses if you're entertaining.

10

PREP

COOK

4

SERVES

party

1 Cut the melon in half and remove and discard the seeds.

2 In a blender or food processor, blend the melon flesh until smooth. Season to taste with salt and pepper.

3 Finely dice 4 of the ham slices and stir into the soup. Cut the remaining 4 ham slices into thin ribbons.

4 Serve the soup in chilled bowls, garnished with the ham ribbons and torn basil leaves.

1 ripe **cantaloupe melon** or **charentais melon**, about 3 lb

8 slices of **prosciutto**

salt and **pepper**

red basil leaves, torn, to garnish

index

Executive Editor Nicky Hill

Editor Charlotte Macey

Executive Art Editor Darren Southern

Designer Ginny Zeal

Senior Production Controller Manjit Sihra